Contents

Line references in these Notes are to the
Arden Shakespeare: A Midsummer Night's Dream,
but as references are given to particular acts
and scenes, the Notes may be used with any
edition of the play.

General editor: Graham Handley MA Ph.D.

Brodie's Notes on William Shakespeare's

A Midsummer Night's Dream

T. W. Smith BA
Former English teacher, Barrow and Teignmouth Grammar Schools

WITHDRAWN

MACMILLAN

First edition published 1985
by Pan Books Ltd
Revised edition 1990

Published by
MACMILLAN PRESS LTD
Houndmills, Basingstoke, Hampshire RG21 6XS
and London
Companies and representatives
throughout the world

ISBN 0–333–58175–X

This book is printed on paper suitable for recycling and
made from fully managed and sustained forest sources.

10   9   8   7   6   5   4   3
04   03   02   01   00   99   98   97   96

Printed in Great Britain by
Mackays of Chatham PLC
Chatham, Kent

Preface

This student revision aid is based on the principle that in any close examination of Shakespeare's plays 'the text's the thing'. Seeing a performance, or listening to a tape or record of a performance, is essential and is in itself a valuable and stimulating experience in understanding and appreciation. However, a real evaluation of Shakespeare's greatness, of his universality and of the nature of his literary and dramatic art, can only be achieved by constant application to the texts of the plays themselves. These revised editions of Brodie's Notes are intended to supplement that process through detailed critical commentary.

The first aim of each book is to fix the whole play in the reader's mind by providing a concise summary of the plot, relating it back, where appropriate, to its source or sources. Subsequently the book provides a summary of each scene, followed by *critical comments*. These may convey its importance in the dramatic structure of the play, creation of atmosphere, indication of character development, significance of figurative language etc, and they will also explain or paraphrase difficult words or phrases and identify meaningful references. At the end of each act revision questions are set to test the student's specific and broad understanding and appreciation of the play.

An extended critical commentary follows this scene by scene analysis. This embraces such major elements as characterization, imagery, the use of blank verse and prose, soliloquies and other aspects of the play which the editor considers need close attention. The paramount aim is to send the reader back to the text. The book concludes with a series of revision questions which require a detailed knowledge of the play; the first of these has notes by the editor of what *might* be included in a written answer. The intention is to stimulate and to guide; the whole emphasis of this commentary is to encourage the student's *involvement* in the play, to develop disciplined critical responses and thus promote personal enrichment through the imaginative experience of our greatest writer.

Graham Handley

Shakespeare and the Elizabethan playhouse

William Shakespeare was born in Stratford-upon-Avon in 1564, and there are reasons to suppose that he came from a relatively prosperous family. He was probably educated at Stratford Grammar School and, at the age of eighteen, married Anne Hathaway, who was twenty-six. They had three children, a girl born shortly after their marriage, followed by twins in 1585 (the boy died in 1596). It seems likely that Shakespeare left for London shortly after a company of visiting players had visited Stratford in 1585, for by 1592 – according to the jealous testimony of one of his fellow-writers Robert Greene – he was certainly making his way both as actor and dramatist. The theatres were closed because of the plague in 1593; when they reopened Shakespeare worked with the Lord Chamberlain's men, later the King's Men, and became a shareholder in each of the two theatres with which he was most closely associated, the Globe and the Blackfriars. He later purchased New Place, a considerable property in his home town of Stratford, to which he retired in 1611; there he entertained his great contemporary Ben Jonson (1572–1637) and the poet Michael Drayton (1563–1631). An astute businessman, Shakespeare lived comfortably in the town until his death in 1616.

This is a very brief outline of the life of our greatest writer, for little more can be said of him with certainty, though the plays – and poems – are living witness to the wisdom, humanity and many-faceted nature of the man. He was both popular and successful as a dramatist, perhaps less so as an actor. He probably began work as a dramatist in the late 1580s, by collaborating with other playwrights and adapting old plays, and by 1598 Francis Meres was paying tribute to his excellence in both comedy and tragedy. His first original play was probably *Love's Labour's Lost* (1590) and while the theatres were closed during the plague he wrote his narrative poems *Venus and Adonis* (1593) and *The Rape of Lucrece* (1594). The sonnets were almost certainly written in the 1590s, though not published until 1609; the first 126 seem to be addressed to a young man who was his friend and patron, while the rest are concerned with the 'dark lady'.

The dating of Shakespeare's plays has exercised scholars ever since the publication of the First Folio (1623), which listed them as comedies, histories and tragedies. It seems more important to look at them chronologically as far as possible, in order to trace Shakespeare's considerable development as a dramatist. The first period, say to the middle of the 1590s, included such plays as *Love's Labour's Lost*, *The Comedy of Errors*, *Richard III*, *The Taming of the Shrew*, *Romeo and Juliet* and *Richard II*. These early plays embrace the categories listed in the First Folio, so that Shakespeare the craftsman is evident in his capacity for variety of subject and treatment. The next phase includes *A Midsummer's Night's Dream*, *The Merchant of Venice*, *Henry IV Parts 1 and 2*, *Henry V* and *Much Ado About Nothing*, as well as *Julius Caesar*, *As You Like It* and *Twelfth Night*. These are followed, in the early years of the 17th century, by his great tragic period: *Hamlet*, *Othello*, *King Lear* and *Macbeth*, with *Antony and Cleopatra* and *Coriolanus* belonging to 1607–09. The final phase embraces the romances (1610–13), *Cymbeline*, *The Tempest* and *The Winter's Tale* and the historical play *Henry VIII*.

Each of these revision aids will place the individual text under examination in the chronology of the remarkable dramatic output that spanned twenty years from the early 1590s to about 1613. The practical theatre for which Shakespeare wrote and acted derived from the inn courtyards in which performances had taken place, the few playhouses in his day being modelled on their structure. They were circular or hexagonal in shape, allowing from the balconies and boxes around the walls full view of the stage. This large stage, which had no scenery, jutted out into the pit, the most extensive part of the theatre, where the poorer people – the 'groundlings' – stood. There was no roof (though the Blackfriars, used from 1608 onwards, was an indoor theatre) and thus bad weather meant no performance. Certain plays were acted at court, and these private performances normally marked some special occasion. Costumes, often rich ones, were used, and music was a common feature, with musicians on or under the stage; this sometimes had additional features, for example a trapdoor to facilitate the entry of a ghost. Women were barred by law from appearing on stage, and all female parts were played by boy actors; this undoubtedly explains the

many instances in Shakespeare where a woman has to conceal her identity by disguising herself as a man, e.g. Rosalind in *As You Like It*, Viola in *Twelfth Night*.

Shakespeare and his contemporaries often adapted their plays from sources in history and literature, extending an incident or a myth or creating a dramatic narrative from known facts. They were always aware of their own audiences, and frequently included topical references, sometimes of a satirical flavour, which would appeal to – and be understood by – the groundlings as well as their wealthier patrons who occupied the boxes. Shakespeare obviously learned much from his fellow dramatists and actors, being on good terms with many of them. Ben Jonson paid generous tribute to him in the lines prefaced to the First Folio of Shakespeare's plays:

Thou art a monument without a tomb,
And art alive still, while thy book doth live
And we have wits to read, and praise to give.

Among his contemporaries were Thomas Kyd (1558–94) and Christopher Marlowe (1564–93). Kyd wrote *The Spanish Tragedy*, the revenge motif here foreshadowing the much more sophisticated treatment evident in *Hamlet*, while Marlowe evolved the 'mighty line' of blank verse, a combination of natural speech and elevated poetry. The quality and variety of Shakespeare's blank verse owes something to the innovatory brilliance of Marlowe, but carries the stamp of individuality, richness of association, technical virtuosity and, above all, the genius of imaginative power.

The texts of Shakespeare's plays are still rich sources for scholars, and the editors of these revision aids have used the Arden editions of Shakespeare, which are regarded as pre-eminent for their scholarly approach. They are strongly recommended for advanced students, but other editions, like The New Penguin Shakespeare, The New Swan, The Signet are all good annotated editions currently available. A reading list of selected reliable works on the play being studied is provided at the end of each commentary and students are advised to turn to these as their interest in the play deepens.

Literary terms used in these notes

Simile The discovery of a striking resemblance between two objects otherwise quite different from each other, introduced by 'like' or 'as'. The second, which is usually familiar, throws new and often picturesque light on the first. Similes in the play are relatively few, but effective. To Theseus the old moon is like a dowager thwarting an expectant heir; to Hippolyta the new moon, shaped like the bow with which she is expert, will be a spectator – to more, indeed, than she anticipates. In the same scene Lysander likens the brevity of true love (prophetically in his case) in a quadruple simile to: a fugitive sound; a passing shadow; a vanished dream; a flash of lightning, the last being developed into an epic (extended) simile. At the end of Act II Scene 2 he carries the two ill-assorted similes of his former love (a surfeit of sweet food and an abandoned religious heresy) forward into their literal personification in the sleeping form he now hates and deserts.

Metaphor Essentially this is a condensed simile, a comparison without using 'like' or 'as': the second object is substituted for the first (e.g. 'the rose distill'd', for the maiden that marries). There are very few poetical metaphors in the play.

Personification An inanimate object, an idea or a quality is spoken of as if it were a person: 'the moon . . . pale in her anger' (II, 1, 103–4); 'tongue-tied simplicity' (V, 1, 104). In Elizabethan days the above three figures of speech often became far-fetched 'conceits', i.e. clever but artificial expressions: 'this seal of bliss', namely Helena's hand (III, 2, 144).

Alliteration The repetition of initial consonants close together: 'In maiden meditation, fancy-free' (II, 1, 164).

Anachronism A reference to something not in existence at the time. Less noticeable in Shakespeare's time, there are several examples in his plays: 'the gun's report' (III, 2, 22).

Antithesis The balancing of two opposing ideas or contrasting expressions in the same clause or in parallel sentences, thus emphasizing the difference. It could be exaggerated and artificial, as in the fashionable 'Euphuism' of the day, from *Euphues: the Anatomy of Wit* a 'romance' by John Lyly. Mocked by Shakespeare, Euphuism appears in passages like Demetrius's explanation contrasting his 'sickness' when out of love with Helena with his 'health' when he returned to his old love. Cf. also II, 2, 45–51.

Climax The arrangement of three or more ideas in ascending order of importance, e.g. Theseus's description of lunatic, lover and poet (V, 1, 7–17). An anti-climax (bathos) occurs when the last is ridiculous

instead of impressive, e.g. 'O Night, which ever art when day is not'
(V, 1, 169).

Irony The meaning is expressed in words that seem to signify the exact
opposite (one form of sarcasm) e.g. 'a manly enterprise' (III, 2, 157); the
word is derived from the Greek *eironeia*, pretended ignorance.

Dramatic irony is the utterance of a character on stage who is unaware
that the reverse is true, e.g. 'he loves not you' (III, 2, 136).

Periphrasis A roundabout way of describing something in more words
than are necessary, often for poetic effect, e.g. 'night's swift dragons cut
the clouds full fast', i.e. day is breaking (III, 2, 379); 'when Phoebe doth
behold/Her silver visage in the wat'ry glass' i.e. moonlight (I, 1, 209).

Tautology Repetition of the same word or of the same idea in different
words, usually for emphasis e.g. 'From our debate, from our dissension'
(II, 1, 116); 'Your buskin'd mistress and your warrior love' (II, 1, 71).
When not intentional tautology weakens the style.

One form of tautology quite noticeable in this play is the device of
associating words from the same root:

hatred is so far from jealousy
To sleep by hate (IV, 1, 143);

to love unlov'd (III, 2, 234);

thy fair virtue's force perforce doth move me (III, 1, 135);

Their sense thus weak, lost with their fears thus strong,
Made senseless things begin to do them wrong (III, 2, 27).

Another kind of repetition is a favourite trick of Shakespeare's: the
frequent reference to a key word or symbol, e.g. *honour* in *Julius Caesar*
and *blood* in *Macbeth*. Here it is eyesight and the consequent vision:
Hermia wishes her father saw with her eyes; to Helena these same eyes
are 'lode-stars'; Puck's tricks are deceptions of the eye; Lysander reads
love stories in Helena's eyes.

Rhythm (Measured movement) in verse or prose is created when a
certain arrangement of stressed and unstressed syllables satisfies the
ear. It helps a poet to communicate emotion.

Metre Defines the rhythm of each line of verse by the number and
nature of its 'feet':

iambic (×/) two syllables with the stress on the second;
trochaic (/×) two syllables with the stress on the first;
anapaestic (××/) three syllables with the stress on the last;
dactylic (/××) three syllables with the stress on the first.

A 'verse', now usually employed for a group of 'lines', was originally a
single line which 'turned' (from Latin *versus*) at a particular point for the
beginning of a fresh line. The bulk of English verse and of
Shakespeare's plays is in *iambic pentameters* (five feet). The second metre,
trochaic, is used mostly in lines of seven or eight syllables (octosyllabic).
Its lilting effect is suited to fairy songs, incantations and dances:

Í dŏ wánđer éverўwhére.

Hence there is more of this metre in the *Dream* than in any other play by Shakespeare.

Rhyme (Strictly 'rime', mis-spelt through confusion with 'rhythm') is the agreement (sometimes approximate) in sound of the final syllables of two or more lines. Much of Shakespeare's early work is in rhymed couplets, with occasional quatrains, rhyming ABAB. In our play there are changes, blank verse to rhymed and back again, not always with a clear reason – perhaps it depended on the author's mood! Rhyme may mark passages that are lyrical, passionate or very artificial. Oberon invites Titania to the dance with eight lines, all rhyming in long 'e', and he applies the juice to Demetrius with another eight all ending in long 'i'.

Stress variation If the stress fell regularly on the second syllable of each iambic foot the effect would, of course, be very monotonous. In good verse it moves frequently to the first syllable, especially in the first foot:

Knów oⱡ yŏur youth, ex̆amĭne well yoŭr blóod.

The placing of the *caesura* (pause) in different parts of the line instead of at the end also brings flexibility.

It is also worth noting that all five stresses in a pentameter are not of equal weight. Characteristic of Shakespeare are the changes rung on three major and two minor stresses (the study of these should help in preparing to speak the longer passages):

But eárthlier happy is the róse distíll'd
Than that which withering on the vírgin thórn
Gróws, líves and díes in síngle blessedness.

Use of prose Pentameter verse is the normal form of Shakespeare's dialogue.

When prose is used it is for a definite purpose:

(1) By comic characters like Bottom;

(2) By characters of lower social position, including middle-class citizens. (*The Merry Wives of Windsor* is almost entirely in prose). In the *Dream* the prose colloquialisms and bad grammar of the mechanicals contrast with the rhythmical utterances of lovers and fairies. Compare one reaction on waking: 'These things seem small and undistinguishable,/Like far-off mountains turned into clouds.' with another: 'God's my life, stolen hence, and left me asleep.' Some of Shakespeare's characters speak, according to the occasion, in verse or prose. After all the emotion of the blank and rhymed verse scenes, Theseus and his court relax into prose for their quips at the turgid couplets and quatrains uttered by Bottom and company essaying high drama in verse.

The play

Plot

Theseus, 'Duke' of Athens, has conquered his bride Hippolyta Queen of the Amazons in battle, and promises to make up for such a violent wooing with a wedding feast full of mirth. The night fixed for the festivities is the first of the new moon of May. When Hermia is brought before Theseus by her father Egeus, because she refuses to give up her lover Lysander for her father's preference Demetrius, the Athenian ruler fixes the same date for Hermia to make her choice between compliance and either death or a nunnery. Lysander and Hermia flee from Athens to a nearby wood, to which they are pursued by Demetrius (who has been informed of the elopement by Helena whom he has loved and slighted).

In the wood the fairy king and queen – drawn here from the fairy world to bless the wedding – have quarrelled over the possession of a changeling. In order to get his own way, Oberon uses the juice of a magic herb to make Titania fall in love with the first creature of the wood that she beholds on waking. When he sees Helena, who has followed Demetrius, pleading in vain for his love, he orders his messenger Puck, the goblin familiar to English households, to work the same charm on Demetrius. Puck, however, mistakes the sleeping Lysander for Demetrius, and amusing complications ensue, until the tangle is straightened, and Theseus, out hunting in the early morning, finds the problem solved for him by the restoration of Demetrius to Helena.

The same night, half a dozen Athenian craftsmen, working on a play in honour of Theseus's wedding, have met in the wood to rehearse secretly. Puck, in one of his mischievous moods, finds them and, when their chief actor Bottom the weaver returns with an ass's head on his shoulders, the rest scatter in terror. Singing to comfort himself, Bottom awakens Titania and is straightaway loved by her and given fairies to attend on him. After Oberon has easily obtained his changeling, he releases

Titania from her spell, Puck removes the ass's head, and Bottom returns to Athens in time for the play to be produced at the palace, where the lovers have joined Theseus and Hippolyta in a triple wedding. The farcical performance of *Pyramus and Thisbe* ends the play, except for the dance of the fairies before they bestow their blessings.

Sources

Shakespeare rarely troubled to invent a story: either he had not the gift or there were more than sufficient books to draw upon. His collected plays reflect the remarkable width and variety of his reading – history, poetry, plays, fiction, all came as grist to his mill. Evidence, both in textual coincidence and similarity of incident, shows that he found ideas for this play in several works:

1. The 'Life of Theseus' in the *Parallel Lives* by Plutarch (died *c.* AD 140). These biographies of famous Greeks and Romans were popular during the Renaissance and translated from the French version of Amyot by Sir Thomas North in 1579; they were used by Shakespeare for his Roman plays. There are accounts of two battles fought by Theseus with the Amazons, in one of which he captured Antiopa (II, 1, 80), and in the other Hippolyta. Besides Egeus, properly the father of Theseus himself, there are references to Ariadne, Aegle and Perigouna (II, 1, 78–80);

2. *The Nun's Priest's Tale* in Chaucer's *Canterbury Tales*, which makes Hippolyta the bride of 'Duke' Theseus, whose niece has rival lovers in Palamon and Arcite. They are discovered in the act of fighting each other in a wood outside Athens by Theseus and Hippolyta, out hunting on the first morning of May. (Philostrate was the pseudonym adopted by Arcite in disguise.);

3. The *Metamorphoses* of the Roman love poet Ovid (*c.* 43 BC – AD 17) translated by Arthur Golding (1565) to which work Shakespeare owed much material from classical myths. It includes the story, based in Babylon, of Pyramus and Thisbe. Here we find the cranny in the wall, Ninus's tomb and the mulberry tree. Beneath this tree was a spring, at which a lioness, with blood on her from killing cattle, came to drink, leaving

paw-marks. When the frightened Thisbe fled to a distant cave, the lioness tore her mantle to pieces. Pyramus, finding Thisbe's blood-stained mantle, assumed she was dead and stabbed himself. On finding him Thisbe too stabbed herself to death. The blood spouting from the lovers' breasts turned the fruit of the mulberry from white to black! There were other versions of the story, some in the extravagant language ridiculed by Shakespeare;

4. *The Boke of Duke Huon of Burdeaux*, a translation (1534) by Lord Berners of an early French romance, which has an Oberon as the three-foot-high king of 'the fairie' in Momur, in or near India; he is able to cover great distances in the space of seconds (more appropriate to him than to the English Puck). The name is from the French Auberon, itself derived from the German Alberich (meaning 'elf-king'), a dwarf in the *Nibelungenlied*. Huon chose to travel by a shorter road, although it meant traversing a wood sixteen leagues in length, where this Oberon had in his power any who spoke in answer to his pleasing speeches. The Fairy king also had a magic horn which could restore weary travellers. The name Titania seems to have been taken direct from the original Latin of Ovid;

5. *Diana*, a Spanish prose romance by Jorge de Montemayor, of which there is a translation by Bartholomew Young, first printed in 1598, but possibly circulating in manuscript some years before. In it the love of a shepherd is changed by a charm;

6. Reginald Scot's *Discoverie of Witchcraft* (1584), an attack on popular superstitions, which gives a description of Robin Goodfellow's domestic activities, such as sweeping the house at midnight, and refers to transportation by the fairies and to the witches' power of turning men into asses. Puck (from Old Norse *puki*, mischievous demon), was originally a general term for 'goblin', and the 'hob' of hobgoblin is an abbreviation of Robin. Long after Shakespeare's day travellers were 'pixie-led' on Dartmoor, and Hampshire horses decoyed into bogs by the neighing of 'colt-pixies' (see II, 1, 45–6). Robin's reaction when offended by finding clothes charitably laid out for him was said to be:

'What have we here? Hemton and Hamton, here will I never more/tread nor stampen? (See III, 1, 75, III, 2, 25 and note).

Scot's phrase 'the illusion and knaverie of Robin goodfellow' also seems to be echoed in III, 2, 346.

Treatment

From these varied sources Shakespeare could have taken the elements he fancied and woven them into a balanced organic whole, his own contribution being the addition of Helena to make a four-square lovers' quarrel, the real climax of the comedy. In the process he has turned the armed quarrel into a matter of bitter words only, thanks to the magic of fairies who themselves have shed much that was sinister in contemporary belief. Nowhere is Shakespeare's sense of fun more entertaining or more kindly. At the end of a day of misunderstanding all is reconciliation and celebration. Bottom has excelled himself and the audience's mockery is good-natured. The theatre audience in its turn has happily whiled away two good hours.

Text and date of the play

Few readers of Shakespeare realize the difficulties that scholars have had to overcome in order to establish accurate texts of the plays. The First Folio, not published until seven years after Shakespeare's death, contained thirty-six plays. Other collected editions or Folios were published in the seventeenth century, the Third and Fourth Folios containing seven additional plays, none of which, with the exception of *Pericles*, is now thought to be by Shakespeare. Sixteen of the plays had already been published separately as Quartos before 1623 and in the case of *A Midsummer Night's Dream* two Quarto editions were printed in 1600, within five years of the first presentation of the play, which must have been subsequent to the disastrous summer of 1594, graphically described in Act II Scene 1. The text of the play is thus very reliable. Both the Quarto editions (one in particular) are almost word for word the same as the text in the First Folio and were possibly set up from Shakespeare's own manuscript or at least from accurate theatre copies.

Quarto editions of some of the plays are shortened inferior versions, however, possibly 'pirated' editions published by some unauthorized person who had access to theatre copies or parts of them, or who had taken down the plays in shorthand while they were being performed. It is thought that the texts of the First Folio were set up from the good Quartos and from good theatre copies. But these texts must all be compared, printers' mistakes and other interference traced, before a reliable text can be arrived at. The first editor to attempt the problem of the text was Nicholas Rowe (1674–1718), who also divided most of the plays into acts and scenes, supplied place-names of the location of each scene, indications of entrances and exits and a list of dramatis personae, which are absent from many of the texts in the Quarto and Folio editions. In *A Midsummer Night's Dream* all the acts but no scenes are marked in the First Folio; the entrances of the characters are almost as in our modern editions and the great majority of the exits. Rowe's divisions are convenient for reference (like the division of the books of the

Bible into chapters and verse) but have no important use in Shakespearian study. They were fitted for the stage of his time, but were unnecessary upon Shakespeare's open stage with the barest of scenery.

Scene summaries, critical commentary, textual notes and revision questions

Act I Scene 1

In the first three scenes of the play the three groups of characters are in turn introduced and their relations to each other within these groups made clear. The three plots are also set in motion without delay, their action having a common centre in the wedding of Theseus and Hippolyta.

The approaching ceremony furnishes the framework of the play, and its brief announcement in the opening lines strikes the keynote of beguiling the time with revels. The warrior 'duke', having won his bride by conquest, calls for entertainment in her honour; unknown to him the fairy world has also regarded the occasion as one requiring their special blessing. The revels in both worlds, however, are interrupted by quarrels which, through the influence of a magic juice in the moonlit glades of an enchanted wood, assume the character of a fantastic dream full of midsummer madness.

First the Athenian duke has to leave the theme of his own wedding to give judgement on a love-tangle in a city whose laws allow a father to dispose of his child in marriage as he pleases. Old Egeus protests that his daughter Hermia will not consent to marry Demetrius, the man he has chosen for her, and accuses Lysander, with whom she is in love, of having stolen her affection by giving her presents; he demands her death if she will not obey him.

Theseus warns her that if she refuses to wed Demetrius she must either die or enter a nunnery. As she will not change her mind, he gives her until his own wedding-day to choose. When Lysander declares that Demetrius has already loved and deserted another woman, Helena, the Duke recollects the fact but declares that even he cannot break the law. He takes Egeus and Demetrius with him to give them instructions about the forthcoming festivities, and leaves the lovers together.

After they have bemoaned their unhappy position Lysander proposes to Hermia that they should flee the city to meet in the wood where they had met once before, and should go for refuge to a wealthy aunt of his. Then Helena appears, reproaching Hermia's beauty for the inconstancy of her lover, and they try to comfort her by revealing their plan. Left to herself, Helena ungratefully decides to inform Demetrius of their flight, in order to win some slight favour in his eyes.

Commentary

Like an overture this opening scene sets the pattern, the pace and the poetic style of the play: falling in and out of love, with the quarrels that ensue; wedding festivities interrupted by a marriage case up for judgement; fierce arguments alternating with finely worded passages, on the bleakness of a nun's life or the transitoriness of love. Here is plotted the escape from the harsh world of reality into that other world of fantasy, the woodland by moonlight, where earthly pursuit may be avoided but where another power, supernatural magic, exerts its influence, something other than 'faint primrose-beds'.

It is Helena who has the last word at this stage: her desperate plight has aroused the sympathy of the theatre audience (and readers) as they hear her eloquent denunciation of the winged boy-god Cupid whose use, when blindfold, of his bow and arrows plays tricks on poor mortals. Her bitter words make the pretty oath just uttered by Hermia seem something easily forsworn. It is, of course, Puck, with his impish 'mistakes', accidental and intentional, who is to play the mischievous part of Cupid in the wood where the law of Athens no longer applies, only the goodwill of the fairy folk. Helena's sole aspiration is to be near the lover who scorns her; so she is mad enough to betray her friends' confidence and provoke the confrontation. Already here are the lunacy, the love and the poetry referred to in Theseus's famous speech in Act V – after the fairies have solved his problem for him.

Metrically the scene falls into two parts (because of two different periods of composition, some might say). The blank verse of the court hearing, and consequent preparations for flight, changes at Hermia's elaborate promise (not to fail the rendez-vous) into rhymed pentameters, artificial by comparison, but perhaps more suited to this more intimate discussion of love and its problems. It is to be followed by a swift descent to the earthy prose of 'mine honest neighbours' in the next scene.

our nuptial hour . . . apace Our wedding day is rapidly approaching.

happy Lucky, perhaps, only in leading up to the ceremony – the last few days of some Greek months, especially April, were held to be unlucky. And May was a month to be avoided for marriages (see section on *Setting*).

withering out Reducing the amount (of his wealth, by living on instead of dying and leaving him to inherit the property which has become hers as his father's widow or even his second wife).

dowager Title of the widow of a lord, to distinguish her from her son's wife.

steep themselves i.e. find relief through sleep, as if bathed in soothing liquid.

solemnities Festivites.

pert Lively.

companion A contemptuous word for the sober person (personified in 'melancholy') whose face is pale from too much brooding.

pomp Pageantry, without the modern sense of ostentatious display.

doing thee injuries i.e. while actually wounding thee.

triumph Celebratory procession.

Duke This title, from Latin 'dux' and ranking next to that of 'king', was often misapplied by early writers, e.g. Chaucer.

Thou, thou . . . thou This repetition is insulting. 'Thou' could express either (1) affection or (2) contempt, while 'you' was polite. Later in the play students should note the changes rung on these pronouns in the lovers' speeches (sometimes inconsistently).

faining voice Voice that strives to please (no connection with 'fain', willing).

feigning love Love that is mere pretence.

stol'n the impression of her fantasy Wrongfully made yourself the object of her love.

gauds Showy trifles.

conceits Gifts contrived to please.

Knacks Knick-knacks.

prevailment Influence.

To leave the figure or disfigure it i.e. either leave your shape untouched or destroy it (by execution).

in this kind . . . voice In so far as he lacks your father's approval.

concern Affect.

In such a presence here Before Your Excellency.

Know of Consider.

blood Passion.

a nun The word is an anachronism, as the time is pre-Christian, but there were virgin priestesses throughout classical days.

mew'd i.e. confined, from the cage where a falcon was kept while 'mewing' or moulting.

a barren sister A childless nun. This expression, together with 'shady cloister', 'faint hymns' and 'maiden pilgrimage', belongs to the convent life known to Shakespeare's audience.

fruitless moon Because it is the sun that ripens crops.

earthlier happy Happier in a worldly sense.

distill'd i.e. into scent.

withering on the virgin thorn i.e. dying without producing anything. 'Thorn' originally referred to any bush with thorns, e.g. the rose, but is now used only of the hawthorn.

yield my virgin patent up . . . sovereignty Surrender my title to remain a virgin to the authority (as husband) of one to whom my soul refuses obedience; 'his lordship' = the authority of him.

sealing-day Wedding day, when the signatures of the two partners will be made authentic by seals.

as he would i.e. as Egeus would.

Diana's altar Diana, Roman goddess of chastity, had her altars, but this one would have closer associations, in the spectators' minds, with a convent chapel.

protest Make a solemn declaration.

crazed Unsound, from 'craze' to break into pieces (cf. 'crazy pavement'); it contrasts with 'certain' i.e. well-established.

as well deriv'd Of as good descent.

possess'd Educated (in conduct). His property is referred to in the next line.

If not with vantage i.e. if not actually better off. Is he thinking of *his* dowager aunt, soon to be mentioned, in 1.157?

to his head To his face.

spotted Marked by moral blemishes, e.g. inconstancy in love. Cf. 'spotless reputation'.

self-affairs My own business.

schooling Instructions.

arm yourself Prepare (not with weapons, but by reflection).

extenuate Mitigate, i.e. alter in your favour.

what cheer, my love? Hippolyta has been saddened by the dispute and the thought of the possible consequences.

against In preparation for.

With duty and desire we follow you Surely a hypocritical remark coming from a father unwilling to leave his daughter alone with a forbidden lover! Some critics think two scenes have been joined together here.

How chance How does it happen that . . .

Belike Probably.

Beteem Pour down on (the roses). The intensive prefix 'be-' is still active in word formation: befriend, bemoan.

in blood According to birth i.e. there was a difference in social status.

O cross! . . . O spite! . . . O hell! In this arrangement of alternating single lines, called 'stichomythia' in classical drama, the responding outbursts are a mark of Hermia's passionate nature, to be seen later in the quarrel with Helena.

misgraffed Misfitted. A metaphor from grafting cuttings onto a tree. Did the poet reflect for a moment on his own marriage to a woman eight years older?

to choose love by another's eyes The frequent mention in this scene of the influence of the eyes in choice of partner, as well as the blindness of Cupid, lead up to the power of the magic juice.

a sympathy in choice i.e. the couple were really lovers.

momentany Momentary.

collied Coal-black.

spleen Fit of anger.

unfolds Reveals.

ever cross'd Always thwarted.

edict in destiny Decree of fate.

teach our trial patience i.e. shame fate by showing ourselves examples of patience under suffering.

a customary cross i.e. something to be endured, as under any other 'edict'.

fancy's followers Those who have fallen in love. Poor Hermia has some flat lines inflicted on her, whereas those of Lysander are charged with poetic extravagance.

a dowager . . . hath no child This financial prospect has already been hinted at in lines 101–2. Theseus's 'dowager' was part of a simile.

seven leagues This fairy-tale distance (once covered by giant boots) makes the house 'remote' enough to be in some rival city-state.

respects Looks upon.

without Outside.

observance to a morn of May An old English custom.

golden head The golden-tipped arrows of Cupid, god of love, were supposed to inspire love, the leaden-tipped ones hate.

Venus' doves These birds, symbols of innocence, were sacred to Venus, Roman goddess of love and, according to some myths, mother of Cupid.

the Carthage queen Dido, said by Virgil to have sacrificed herself on a funeral pyre after the departure of Aeneas, the 'false Trojan' with whom she had fallen in love. Actually, this is an anachronism, as Theseus pre-dated Dido.

lode-stars Guiding stars, like the pole-star, by which navigators fixed their direction.

favour Beauty of feature.

bated Excepted.

to you translated Transformed to your likeness.

None but your beauty i.e. the fault lies not with you, but with your beauty. This second use of *stichomythia*, with its balancing of opposites, shows Helena making the passionate responses to Hermia's defensive arguments.

a hell Because in Athens she had been forbidden to see him.

Phoebe The name for Diana in her capacity as goddess of the moon. All three spheres of her divine influence are represented in this play: the moon, chastity and hunting.

still Always.

He will not know . . . know i.e. he refuses to recognize that I am as beautiful as Hermia.

So I So do I (err).

holding no quantity Lacking all proportion.

transpose Transform (by fond imagination). The object 'Things' precedes the verb.

form Fine shape.

of any judgement taste i.e. a scrap of judgement.

figure Represent.

eyne Eyes (old plural).

intelligence Information.

a dear expense Dearly bought (betraying her friend).

to enrich my pain To give sorrow something of value.

his sight The pleasure of seeing him (for a brief moment).

Act I Scene 2

In strong contrast to the emotional susceptibilities of court ladies and gentlemen and their cultured phraseology there follows this scene of the broadest comedy, in which the entirely unconscious humour is almost wholly supplied by one character, Bottom, who asserts himself from the start.

A band of amateur players from the humblest quarter of the city has quickly responded to the duke's request for entertainment. Quince, as producer, proceeds to explain the play and allot the parts. Bottom, not content with the chief part, shows how much better he could play the tyrant than the lover, and then volunteers for two other parts, Thisbe and the Lion, with further demonstrations of his histrionic powers. The players then disperse to meet in secret for a rehearsal in the same wood to which the lovers are to flee.

Commentary

This is a Shakespearian under-plot, often, as here, a comic parallel to the serious main plot. It is linked to the latter by the similar decision: to avoid trouble (in the form of undesirable witnesses of any attempts at rehearsal) the producer names the quite extensive wood outside the city. 'Tomorrow night' (the eve of May) is the time, and a well-known oak the rendezvous. Why did the theatrical party not find it in Act III Scene 2? Was Quince confused by Bottom's contrariness on the way or was he drawn aside by the 'bank where the wild thyme blows' as 'a marvellous convenient place for our rehearshal'? It brings about the link with the other 'under-plot', the dispute between Oberon and Titania.

BOTTOM, *the Weaver* 'A clew on which to wind thread: also a skein or ball of thread' (OED).

You were best You had better.

generally Bottom's first malapropism, for 'individually', contradicting the very next words, 'man by man.'

scrip A small sheet of paper, with the names of the actors on it, not the modern 'script'.

through all Athens An extraordinary statement in a city famous for its drama! Quince's sense of importance, however, is soon to be eclipsed by that of Bottom.

interlude Originally an episode performed during an interval at a banquet, then any short comedy of the sixteenth century.

grow to a point He means 'come to the point'.

Marry Literally 'by the Virgin Mary', but having no more significance than 'Why, to be sure'.

Pyramus and Thisbe See *Sources*, para 3.

condole Mourn.

To the rest i.e. now for the rest of the actors. But he cannot help a further digression on his own capabilities.

tear a cat Make a violent speech.

to make all split i.e. to burst the ear-drums of the audience.

Phibbus' car The chariot of Phoebus, god of the sun.

make and mar Bring prosperity and ruin. The subject is 'fates'.

Ercles' vein The manner of Hercules, a raging character in earlier drama, like Herod in the miracle plays.

bellows-mender He mended the bellows of organs, hence his musical name.

That's all one It does not matter.

small i.e. treble.

Thisbe's mother This and the following two parts are later omitted to make room for others.

nothing but roaring Later changed for a reassuring speech to the audience!

you would fright the Duchess and the ladies In a celebration of the baptism of Prince Henry (elder brother of Charles I, who died young) at the Scottish court in 1594, a lion was to have drawn a car, but the item was cancelled for a similar reason.

aggravate He means 'moderate'.

sucking dove The nestlings of this inoffensive bird were traditionally fed by the parent on 'pigeon's milk'.

proper Handsome.

I will undertake it Bottom succumbs to Quince's flattery.

purple-in-grain Dyed red.

French crown This gold coin was English slang for a bald crown.

entreat . . . request . . . desire In the inverted order of an *anti-climax*.

bill of properties List of stage 'props'.

obscenely Malapropism for 'obscurely'.

courageously Also inappropriate in view of the players' declared fear of premature publicity.

perfect i.e. word-perfect.

the Duke's oak Like any English king or nobleman, Theseus has a tree named after him.

cut bow-strings A punishment to which an archer who failed to turn up at the shooting-range was liable.

Revision questions on Act I

1 Describe clearly the situation and feelings of each of the four lovers.

2 What are your first impressions of Bottom as an actor?

3 What details in this Act can you distinguish as
(a) characteristic of Athens, (b) foreign to it?

4 How many different kinds of love are represented in Act I?

5 Explain the various motives that are to bring the four lovers together in the wood.

Act II Scene 1

The remainder of the play up to Act IV Scene 2 takes place in the 'palace wood'. The following scene introduces the fairies as the privileged spirits of the wood, whose pranks tease poor mortals and whose quarrels derange the seasons. Oberon uses

his magic powers to torment his royal partner, but when he sees
two intruding humans at cross-purposes he endeavours to set
the matter right. The result of the one action exceeds his expectations, the other leads to complications which he cannot
foresee.

Puck explains to one of the fairies the quarrel between their
King and Queen, and then relates some of his tricks. The two
sovereigns encounter each other unexpectedly, and each jumps
to the conclusion that the other is in Athens to bless the wedding
of a former human lover. Titania lays the blame on Oberon for
their quarrels and adds that the winds, their music thus neglec-
ted by the fairies, have brought about a fantastic change of
seasons, flooding the land and rotting the crops, summer being
turned into winter and winter into summer. Oberon retorts that
the fault is hers in refusing to let him have a changeling boy for
his page, but Titania will not part with the boy, because his
mother was once a favourite attendant who died when he was
born (a version differing from that of Puck).

After her departure Oberon reminds Puck of the magic herb,
Love-in-Idleness or Cupid's Flower, which he once showed him,
and bids him fetch it, so that he may make Titania fall in love
with some monster of the wood, and while she is thus pre-
occupied obtain her consent to transfer the boy to him. Scarcely
has Puck gone upon his errand than Helena follows Demetrius
across the stage pleading in vain for his love. Thereupon
Oberon determines to make Demetrius return her love and,
while he goes to find Titania, gives some of the herb to Puck,
now returned, with instructions to apply it to a man wearing
Athenian garments.

Commentary

The preamble (lines 1–57) is compact with information as well as
a skilful creation of the dual 'fairy' atmosphere (classical myth
and rustic folklore). The dainty fairy at once establishes the
diminutive scale of Shakespeare's little people and also paints
vignettes of Puck's nocturnal operations, while he gloats over his
disguises (anticipating later powers of transformation) and
reveals the cause of Oberon's jealousy. The fairy king and queen
avoid at first the real reason for their dispute, thinking up

accusations of former love affairs with the human duke and his bride.

The scene is remarkable for two passages with 'local colour' alien to an Athens setting: (1) a formidable portrayal of English weather at its worst; and (2) what seems to be a recollection of an elaborate masque in some English nobleman's park. Better known is the lyrical description by Oberon of Titania's sleeping quarters, one which needs to be kept in the audience's mind when the next scene starts – traditionally on a bare stage!

There is a distinction between the rhyme of Puck's pranks and the blank verse of the more impressive account of the false summer, of the Indian love lyric and of the escape of the 'fair vestal' from Cupid's dart, with its palpable compliment to the Virgin Queen of a later age. The bitter atmosphere of the unrhymed and unresolved dispute between Helena and Demetrius is sweetened by the tuneful couplets in which Oberon prepares the seduction of both his queen and the perverse Athenian (Demetrius), the latter a sudden impulse resulting from what he has just seen – Helena's unrequited love intrudes on his personal campaign as Egeus's problem has done on Theseus's plans.

Thorough Older form of 'through'.
pale Enclosure, fence. Cf. 'paling'.
the moon's sphere i.e. the sphere in which the moon was fixed. Early astronomers saw the heavens as a series of revolving, concentric, hollow and transparent spheres, in each of which was set the moon or one of the planets. The whole movement was powered by a mysterious 'primum mobile' and revolved around the Earth.
orbs i.e. the 'fairy rings' caused by a fungus – not the feet of dancing fairies.
pensioners Retainers.
favours Gifts.
live their savours Lies their scent.
lob Clown.
passing fell Extremely fierce.
changeling Usually a child left by the fairies in place of the stolen human one; here the stolen human child is referred to.
Knight Boy attendant (the original meaning).
green Open greensward.
fountain clear Spring whose water flows unimpeded or unpolluted or without overhanging shadow-casting bushes.
spangled starlight sheen i.e. (under) the light of the stars shining like spangles.

square Quarrel. Cf. 'to square up to'.

shrewd Mischievous (the original meaning, taken from the shrew, once believed to be vicious).

Robin Goodfellow A complimentary name for one whose actions were to be feared. Cf. 'sweet Puck' below, line 40.

villagery Obsolete collective noun for villages.

Skim milk Remove its top layer of cream. The verb and those following it agree in sense with 'you', whereas grammatically they should be in the third person singular, like 'frights'.

quern Handmill for grinding corn.

bootless . . . churn Make the housewife go on churning until she is out of breath, but the butter still refuses to form. Sometimes it needed the repetition of a charm, 'Come, butter come'.

barm Froth, showing that the drink has fermented.

Mislead night-wanderers i.e. with a 'will-o'-the-wisp', from 'William with a burning wisp of straw'; in marshy places *ignis fatuus*, the flickering light of gas, suggested a mischievous person deluding travellers.

filly foal Young mare.

gossip's bowl This contained a spiced drink, brewed at christenings, one of the ingredients of which was a roasted crab-apple. A 'gossip' was originally a god-parent, the ceremony proving an occasion for chatter.

wither'd dewlap The loose skin hanging round the throat of an aged person.

aunt Old woman of the neighbourhood.

'tailor' Johnson suggested that this expression arose from the victim's resemblance to a squatting tailor as he fell.

waxen i.e. grow louder. A verb with the old plural inflection '–en'.

neeze Sneeze.

room Make room. The shortened line lays emphasis on this word.

Titania A name used for the goddess Diana by Ovid in his *Metamorphoses*.

wanton Flighty person.

in the shape of Corin The incompatibility of the love affairs between fairies and humans (about to be resurrected from the past) is resolved by the fairies ability to transform themselves (cf. Puck as a crab-apple). Corin and Phillida were traditional names of lovers in pastoral poetry.

pipes of corn Flutes of oat straw.

step Limit of travel. The reading 'steppe' would be an unfamiliar word to Elizabethans and is probably a Quarto error.

Amazon i.e. Hippolyta. The Amazons were a mythical race of warrior women.

buskin'd Wearing 'buskins', the high-heeled boots of hunters.

Glance at my credit with Refer slightingly to my reputation over.

Perigouna . . . Aegles . . . Ariadne Names of women mentioned in North's *Plutarch* as earlier loves of Theseus.

Antiopa Another Amazon queen, sometimes confused with Hippolyta.

middle summer's spring i.e. early summer. 'Spring' originally meant 'beginning' (of the year).

paved fountain Spring with a bed of pebbles.

beached margent Sandy stretch of sea-shore.

ringlets Small circles (danced on by fairies).

contagious Pestilent.

pelting Paltry.

continents Banks, lit. 'containers'.

in vain i.e. the ploughed land has been flooded.

lost his sweat Toiled for nothing.

his youth i.e. the immaturity of the corn (which rots before ripening).

beard The 'awn' or bristly part of oats or barley. There is a pun on the beard of a grown man.

murrion flock Sheep killed by murrain: strictly a disease of cattle.

nine-men's-morris A game played on a diagram of three concentric squares with nine men or pins on each side, the object being to get three of these in a row.

quaint i.e. cunning, ingenious.

mazes Figures cut in the turf of the village green for country dancing. They would be kept in condition by the tread of the dancers.

wanton green Greensward allowed to grow unchecked. Cf. 'wanton' above, line 63.

human mortals What seems to be *tautology* is contrasted in Titania's mind with 'fairy immortals'.

want their winter here Miss their usual winter in this place. The confusion of seasons has spread from a bad summer to a mild unhealthy winter. 'Cheer' has been suggested for 'here' in view of the next line.

washes i.e. fills with moisture.

distemperature Upsetting of the elements.

in the fresh lap of the crimson rose *Periphrasis* for 'in summer'. The opposite phenomenon, rose in winter, is seen in the following lines.

Hiems' A *personification* of the Latin word for winter.

thin i.e. balding.

childing Fruitful.

mazed Puzzled. Cf. 'mazes' above, line 99.

By their increase, now knows not Cannot tell by their products.

debate Quarrel.

henchman Page.

Set your heart at rest i.e. stop craving the impossible.

votress Now spelt 'votaress', one who has taken a vow, e.g. a nun, belonging to an 'order'. If Titania's followers were, like some of Diana's, vowed to celibacy, there may be an infringement of the rules here, but as Lucina, Diana was also goddess of childbirth.

embarked traders Loaded vessels under full sail.

wanton Sportive, gusty, as it 'bellies out' the sails. The third use of this word in the same scene.

my young squire i.e. Titania's infant page.

sail upon the land i.e. trip smoothly along, in her pregnant condition 'imitating' the well-filled sails.

being mortal i.e. a fairy would not have died.

spare your haunts i.e. not offend you with my presence.

chide Scold, quarrel. Hence any strident sound like the barking of hounds (IV, 1, 114).

Since When.

dulcet Sweet.

shot madly from their spheres See note on line 7. This poetical extravaganza, introducing the 'little western flower', may owe something to Shakespeare's recollection of a masque.

thou couldst not Puck, being earthbound, could listen to a mermaid but not follow the aerial manoeuvres of gods.

arm'd i.e. with his bow and arrows.

vestal Priestess in ancient Rome.

might Could.

imperial votress Sovereign virgin. Queen Elizabeth was entertained at nearby Kenilworth Castle in 1575, when Shakespeare was a boy, with pageantry which included a mermaid and a dolphin as well as fireworks.

In maiden meditation, fancy-free i.e. musing, unmarried, and infatuated with nobody. Note the alliteration in this often quoted line.

bolt Arrow.

love-in-idleness Another name for heartsease, a wild pansy.

that flower; the herb These were not so sharply distinguished as they are today.

or ... or Either ... or.

leviathan Whale.

I'll put a girdle ... minutes I'll make the circuit of the world in under an hour (in order to locate and identify a tiny plant he has been shown once!) The number 40 has always had a sacred significance, especially, of course, forty days.

watch Titania when Follow Titania until.

the soul of love Love at its most intense. Cf. 'with heart and soul.'

Another herb Named 'Dian(a)'s bud' in IV, 1, 72.

I am invisible. A reminder to the audience.

conference Talk.

wood within ... wood Mad (long obsolete). Demetrius's habit of punning is more evident in Act V.

hard-hearted adamant This legendary metal (iron) or stone (diamond) had two properties of hardness and magnetism.

you draw not iron i.e. you draw one whose heart is not made of base metal.

leave you Give up.

nor I cannot In Elizabethan English a double negative intensified the idea instead of logically, as today, cancelling it out.

spaniel i.e. a dog that will fawn upon you.

worser Another contemporary form of emphasis is the double comparative.

the hatred of my spirit i.e. my feelings of hatred towards you.

impeach i.e. expose (to danger). Demetrius tries another tack.

To trust the opportunity . . . virginity i.e. to risk yourself at night in a lonely place where evil desires may do you harm.

privilege Special protection.

:for that Because. (Some editors place the colon after 'that'.)

in my respect As I regard you.

brakes Bushes.

Apollo . . . Daphne Daphne, fleeing from the passionate Apollo, appealed to the gods for assistance and was turned by them into a laurel, ever after sacred to his worship.

griffin A mythical monster, half lion, half eagle. Familiar to London citizens as a supporter in their city's coat of arms.

bootless speed Useless haste.

stay thy questions Wait for thy arguments.

do not believe/But You may be sure.

upon the hand At the hand of him whom.

blows Flowers.

oxlips Natural hybrids of cowslips and primroses.

grows Agreement with nearest subject only.

musk-roses Probably wild roses and not the cultivated ones.

luscious woodbine i.e. scented honeysuckle.

eglantine Sweet-briar.

weed Garment (not a wild flower).

streak Draw a streak across.

hateful fantasies Hateful objects to be in love with.

Athenian garments There are more than one dressed thus.

ere the first cock crow i.e. before the night ends – for fairies particularly.

Act II Scene 2

In her own secret bower, near a green glade and hawthorn bush (see III, 1), Titania is sung to sleep by a fairy lullaby, a sleep that is undisturbed by the incidents of this scene and the next, until she is awakened by Bottom's attempts to sing. Oberon now enters and squeezes the juice on her eyelids. Lysander and Hermia arrive, weary, having lost their way. They lie down at a little distance from each other. Puck, mistaking Lysander for Demetrius, owing to his Athenian garments and the fact that the two are sleeping apart, anoints his eyelids. At this point Demetrius appears again, still pursued by Helena, but he finally forces her to stay there while he makes his way alone in search of the lovers, at that moment asleep but a few feet from him. Catching sight of Lysander (but not of Hermia), Helena wakens him, to be greeted immediately by a fervent protestation of love for her, which she takes for mockery and flees. Pausing to cast scorn upon Hermia, he sets off after Helena. Hermia awakens from a frightening dream to find that Lysander is no longer with her.

Commentary

The last scene was a preparation for action; this is the 'entanglement' or involvement of the main characters in the plot. There are several exits and entrances; two people fall asleep and wake startled. While Titania sleeps on in (probably) the inner stage, space is needed for Lysander to sleep apart from Hermia and for Helena to chase Demetrius without either stumbling over the sleepers.

It resounds with rhyme: iambic five-foot lines, trochaic four-foot lines, treble rhymes; and Lysander achieves a quatrain. The couplets are the right framework for the artificiality of Helena's self-deprecation as a 'monster' and Lysander's extravagant praise of her beauty; they also intensify the pathos of Hermia's desperate exclamations.

roundel As it is mentioned with a song, this is here presumably a dance.
cankers Grubs.
rere mice Bats.
quaint Dainty.
Thorny Spiny.
Newts and blind-worms Then believed to be venomous. 'Blind-worms' means slow-worms.
Philomel In Greek mythology she was saved from death by being turned into a nightingale.
ounce Lynx.
pard Leopard.
In thy eye that shall appear Whatever you catch sight of.
tarry for the comfort Wait for the comforting daylight.
take the sense . . . of my innocence Grasp my innocent meaning (which I have been unable to express).

Love takes the meaning . . . conference Lovers understand each other without the aid of language.

much beshrew Alas for.

So far be distant This piece of maidenly decorum is very necessary to the action of the play; Puck misunderstands the 'distance' between the lovers.

With half that wish . . . press'd i.e. may Lysander have his half-share of the rest that sleep gives.

approve Test.

owe Possess.

darkling In the dark.

fond chase Foolish pursuit.

the lesser is my grace The less I get in answer. 'Lesser' is another double comparative.

wheresoe'er she lies A remarkable piece of dramatic irony.

as a monster As if I were a monster.

sphery eyne Starry eyes.

Nature shows art i.e. this transparency is a clever device of Nature's. An extravagant way of saying that he knows her real feelings.

Do not say so The alarmed Helena, as always, thinks of Demetrius first.

a raven for a dove A brunette for a blonde.

The will of man . . . maid Notice the unconscious irony of this in the mouth of one just swayed by fairy juice!

till now ripe not Have not matured till now. 'Ripe' in the previous line is an adjective, here a verb, 'ripen'.

touching now . . . human skill Reaching at last the height of human wisdom.

marshal i.e. in charge of (ushering in) his 'will'.

o'erlook Read.

nor never Double negative for emphasis.

flout my insufficiency Mock my lack of attractiveness by pretended admiration.

troth . . . sooth Loyalty and truth are used in exclamation, as in 'good heavens!'

gentleness Breeding, gentility.

as the heresies . . . deceive i.e. those who change their religion are the bitterest enemies of their former beliefs.

my surfeit and my heresy The two similes are now transposed into metaphors.

the most of me! By me the most of all!

address your love and might He is speaking to his own faculties.

you sat smiling Dramatic irony, since Lysander has deserted her.

his cruel prey Its cruel preying on me.

and if These words were often used together, although they both mean 'if'.

of all loves In the name of all who have loved.

Revision questions on Act II

1 What picture of fairy life and activity is given in this Act?
2 Describe a rural scene in Shakespeare's day from hints provided in this Athenian wood.
3 Explain the surprises with which the two women meet, and state their reactions.
4 If Lysander had been Demetrius and Demetrius Lysander, do you think they would have acted in the same way?
5 In what ways does the dramatist keep the impression of night before the audience? (Remember that an Elizabethan play took place in daylight.)

Act III Scene 1

The actors in the village play now reach the same spot and proceed with their rehearsal. They have scarcely begun, however, when two serious objections have to be met, Bottom saying a great deal about both. First, the ladies of the prospective audience will not endure the shedding of blood, so a prologue must explain everything beforehand; they will be terrified of a lion, so, as even a prologue is not enough for this, the actor must show himself through the skin and tell the spectactors who he really is.

The producer then propounds his own difficulties: (a) how to get a moonlight effect; (b) how to bring a wall into the duke's banqueting-chamber. The first is to be solved, in default of the moon obliging by shining through an open casement, by one of them representing it with a lamp and thorn-bush. The second difficulty is removed by selecting another actor to appear in a coat of plaster and hold up two fingers for the cranny. Although no reference is made to it, these alterations mean that three characters are dropped out of the original cast: Quince plays Prologue instead of Thisbe's father, Starveling plays Moonshine instead of Thisbe's mother, and Snout plays Wall instead of Pyramus's father.

Then the rehearsal begins, with Puck as sole and invisible spectator. The text of the play, as performed before Theseus, differs entirely from the fragment here presented, but what follows is enough to drive out of their heads not only what they have committed to their shallow memories, but all thought of further play-acting (perhaps the scripts were abandoned in their flight!). They are dispersed in terror by one of Shakespeare's greatest comic inventions: the reappearance of the already sufficiently asinine Bottom with a real ass's head, with its long ears and hairy skin on his shoulders. It has been put there by Puck while 'Pyramus' was off-stage.

Refusing to be discouraged by their panic, he raises his voice in song (it is the same Bottom that speaks through the ass's mouth) in order to display to the fleeing knaves his own composure, thus at last awakening Titania, who is ravished alike by the sweetness of his voice and the handsomeness of his appearance. She summons her attendants and gives them dainty duties to perform for the grotesque object of her new devotion, who proceeds to make their acquaintance in his usual garrulous fashion.

Commentary

At this (the first) part of the wood, just vacated in turn by all four lovers, we reach the climax of both 'under-plots': Oberon's whim and Puck's prank meet in one embrace. This had to precede, not follow, the climax of the main plot. Puck discovers the band of players where he might have expected to find Titania's bodyguard (now out of sight); his action in scaring away the rest of the cast ensures that Titania will see only Bottom on waking.

Curiously the mechanicals show no awareness of their surroundings, except for the bush that serves as a 'tiring-room': the moonlight is merely illumination that must be contrived to shine if and when their play is put on. The shock is all the greater when their leading actor emerges from behind the same bush so 'attired' that they run all the way back to Athens. And they themselves had only just shown so much concern at the possibility of frightening the ladies in the audience with a realistic representation of a lion! Now the same Pyramus who, while earlier coveting the part for himself, had for the same reason been forced to agree to subdue what would have been an impressive roar, is the terrifying object.

Pat i.e. just as arranged and on time.

tiring-house Changing-room, where the actors changed their 'attire'.

bully Originally a complimentary term, like 'friend Bottom'.

Byrlakin By our Ladykin, i.e. little Lady – the Virgin Mary.

a parlous fear A perilous cause of anxiety (they might be punished for it).

when all is done After all.

more better Double comparative, meaning 'even greater'.

such a prologue The Prologue delivered by Quince in Act V differs in being rather more sensible, and composed in decasyllabic instead of octosyllabic verse.

defect He means 'effect'.

it were pity of my life i.e. I should deserve hanging.

into a chamber The production will be inside the palace.

great chamber Such a room, often the largest in the house, is still so-called in some of our older mansions.

a bush of thorns and a lantern Among the shapes to be made out on the moon's surface was a well-known figure, once believed to be the man caught gathering sticks on the Sabbath, as told in Numbers XV, 32–6.

disfigure He means 'figure' or give shape to.

loam In this connection a clayey soil used as a mortar.

hempen home-spuns Wearers of cloth made at home of hemp.

cradle Place of repose.

toward About to take place.

brisky juvenal Lively youth. The script of this playlet satirizes the affected language of some stage productions of this time.

eke Also.

Jew Perhaps suggested by the first syllable of 'juvenal', or merely to rhyme with 'hue'.

I'll meet thee Flute over-runs the cue for Pyramus's return; its repetition heightens the interest with which Bottom is now awaited. Curiously what emerges from the 'tiring-room' is something akin to a horse!

Ninny's tomb A ninny is a simpleton, derived perhaps from 'innocent'. Ninus was the legendary founder of Nineveh. The story was based in Babylon.

If I were fair, Thisbe i.e. even if I were handsome. This unconscious humour is created by his mis-punctuating what must have read in his script: 'If I were (true), fair Thisbe.'

a round A dance.

through bog . . . brier The pronunciation of 'through' and the heavy alliteration of 'b' compensate for this line being two syllables short.

fire i.e. the will o' the wisp. Note how the five sounds are arranged in the correct order.

translated Transformed.

ousel cock Blackbird.

throstle Thrush.

quill The likeliest meaning is 'feather'. Something had to rhyme with 'bill'.

plain-song Singing a simple melody without variations (i.e. two notes).

full many a man Married men were said to be warned in this way of the unfaithfulness of their wives. Cf. note on V, 1, 232.

set his wit to Think of an answer to.

enthralled to thy shape Fascinated by your figure.

thy fair virtue's force perforce doth move me The influence of thy manly excellence necessarily drives me.

you should have little reason for that Is this an unexpected touch of modesty in Bottom?

some honest neighbours i.e. his late companions, whose unreasonable behaviour has estranged him from them.

friends i.e. reason and love.

gleek Jest.

to serve mine own turn i.e. enough wisdom for my own purposes.

of no common rate Of high status.

still doth tend upon my state Is always in attendance on one of my rank.

pressed flowers A kind of *prolepsis* (anticipation): Bottom's bed of flowers is not pressed until he has lain upon it.

mortal grossness This is not a belated realization of Bottom's uncouth figure, but refers to the material substance of his human body as compared with her fairy essence.

Hop in his walks . . . eyes Close attendance by miniature creatures.

apricocks Apricots.

dewberries Strictly blackberries, but, as the other four fruits are products of a cultivated garden, probably gooseberries.

for night-tapers . . . eyes i.e. light tapers of beeswax at the glow made by glow-worms (erroneously believed to come from the eyes instead of the tail). In Shakespeare's day a taper or wax candle would be used to light one up dark stairs.

painted Suggested by the designs painted on real fans used to shade from the rays of the sun (here quaintly replaced by moon beams!).

I cry your worships mercy I humbly beg your pardon (hardly a royal acknowledgement).

I shall desire you of more acquaintance A jumbled version of a formal expression he has heard somewhere.

if I cut my finger Cobwebs were once considered a remedy to stop a cut bleeding.

Squash An unripe pea-pod.

Peascod Pea-pod.

patience i.e. in suffering (explained by what follows).

giant-like i.e. the roast is huge beside the small quantity of mustard.

enforced Violated.
bring him silently The talkative Bottom may betray her obsession to
  Oberon (who has planned it).

Act III Scene 2

Puck describes the previous scene to his master, and also reports
the accomplishment of his own mission, when, to his surprise,
the right woman and the wrong man enter. Hermia suspects
Demetrius of having killed Lysander. When he sulkily confesses
that he knows nothing about him, she leaves him in anger and
he lies down. Oberon blames Puck for making some mistake and
sends him to fetch Helena. He then determines to get one
love-affair straight and anoints Demetrius's eyes in readiness for
Helena, who, however, appears with Lysander at her heels,
threatening a new complication which causes Puck, who has
already mischievously made an ass of Bottom, to gloat over the
folly of these love-struck mortals.

The argument between Lysander and Helena wakens Demetrius, whose spontaneous worship of his former sweetheart is
couched in even more extravagant terms than those used to her
by Lysander and shocks her into thinking herself the victim of a
conspiracy among her friends to mock her. The bickering
between the new lover and the old is leading to threats when the
fourth member of the quartet is guided to the spot by the sound
of voices. Hermia is first perturbed at finding that Lysander has
voluntarily separated himself from her and then amazed to hear
him profess unbounded love for Helena. For her part, Helena
takes her amazement for a part of the plot and upbraids her for
being so untrue to their girlhood friendship.

Lysander's false passion then becomes the centre of the argument. To Helena a changed Demetrius is a remote possibility,
but a changed Lysander as well makes both utterly impossible;
Hermia, whom both have hitherto loved, must be the instigator
of this simultaneous (and simulated) change of heart. Her
desperation leads Hermia to appeal to Lysander and Demetrius to threaten him. The spell is not to be shaken; Lysander
renews his passionate declarations to Helena, challenges Demetrius to fight, and tries to cast off Hermia, who is now clinging to
him, finally telling her that it is not a joke.

Then begins the quarrel between the two women. Hermia calls Helena a thief, and Helena brands Hermia as shameless (in her apparent hypocrisy). When Helena unguardedly refers to her rival's small stature, Hermia threatens to scratch her, tall as she is. Helena then blames her own folly for the quarrel and makes to return to Athens, checked only by unwillingness to leave Demetrius behind. The persistent Lysander offers to champion her, whereupon the two men go off to fight it out. Helena runs from the more shrewish Hermia, who in turn wanders away in despair, leaving the stage to the two unintentional contrivers of the mischief. Puck, while blaming his mistake on the presence of two Athenians in the wood, is quite unrepentant in view of the resulting entertainment. Oberon orders him to create a fog and to separate the duellists further by calling them in different directions; when they fall asleep exhausted he is to squeeze the juice of the other herb on Lysander's eyelids. Meanwhile Oberon will get the boy from Titania and release her from her spell.

Puck plays with Lysander and Demetrius until they lie down near each other; Helena and Hermia also return, one after the other, to sleep till daybreak. Lysander is then disenchanted.

Commentary

In this exceptionally long scene the main plot arrives at its climax, when both lovers are again competing for the favour of the one woman, but not the same one. Hermia and Helena both suffer from this double change of affection; one being mocked, as she thinks, the other being deserted twice over. Worse still, each believes the other to be the cause of her unhappiness and attacks her one-time closest friend, Helena for using her height to her advantage, Hermia for being too vixenish. Helena recoils in fear of Hermia and is instantly offered protection by the two men. If Hermia is the more passionate over losing her lover, Helena is far the more eloquent in her reproaches to all three for their unkind conspiracy to make fun of her. Her picture of the early girlhood friendship thus shattered is very moving. Surprisingly Puck also reveals a gift for description in his account of the rehearsal and its comic result; later he rises to quite a poetical rendering of the impact of daybreak on the spirits of the night.

This second part of the woodland serves for both this scene and the next. In it the producer must place with care his successively recumbent forms (with chalk-marks?) and leave sufficient space for Bottom and Titania to approach (the inner stage?) without tripping over them! The action of the juice on Lysander 'disentangles' the main plot, immediately after its climax and (symmetrically) before the parallel dénouement of the two under-plots to come in the following scene.

in extremity To the extreme.

What night-rule about this haunted grove? Oberon's lofty indirect enquiry into the upshot of what he himself has ordered. 'Night-rule' comes oddly from the 'king of shadows', but 'rule' had a contemporary meaning approximating to 'proceedings', while some critics regard it as a printer's corruption of 'night-revel'. 'Haunted' still had the original sense of 'much frequented by living people' as well as the later restriction to 'visited by apparitions', as used by Quince (III, 1, 99).

close Private.

patches Clowns, in the sense of ignorant workers. Professional clowns wore motley coats of coloured 'patches'.

rude mechanicals Rough artisans.

work for bread i.e. get a living.

thick-skin Thick-head.

barren sort Mindless group.

nole Slang term for the head (from 'knoll').

mimic Actor.

russet-pated choughs Jackdaws with grey heads (contemporary meaning of 'russet').

many in sort In a great company.

the gun's report This is an anachronism.

sever themselves Scatter.

at our stamp Two interpretations: a stage gesture by an actor-sized fairy working his magic; or a tree stump (part of the 'tiring-house'?) over which a single mechanical stumbles (referred to as 'he' in the next line). Cf. IV, 1, 85.

Their sense thus weak . . . wrong The general confusion seems reflected in the expression of these lines, distorted by the demands of rhyme. They might be paraphrased: almost out of their senses and terrified by what they have seen, they begin to think inanimate things are attacking them.

from yielders all things catch Obscure. Perhaps (1) from those who give in everything is torn, or (2) instead of producing fruit (as 'yielders') the bushes seize for themselves (articles of clothing).

latch'd Ensnared. More likely a misprint of 'laced', streaked as with a liquid (cf. Duncan's 'silver skin', in *Macbeth*, 'laced with his golden blood').

of force she must be ey'd i.e. he could not but see her.

close i.e. hidden, but cf. **close** above.

breath Words.

Being o'er shoes Having waded.

displease Her brother's noon-tide Annoy the sun at its height (as it would be in Australia). Phoebe (Diana), goddess of the moon, was in myth sister of Phoebus (Apollo), god of the sun.

Antipodes People living on the opposite side of the earth.

dead Deathly. Demetrius is pale with passion.

Venus Brightest of the planets. For 'sphere', see note on II, 1, 7.

O brave touch! Sarcastically, 'What a courageous act!'

worm Snake.

An adder did it i.e. you killed him. See next line.

with doubler tongue i.e. with greater treachery. The snake was believed to sting its victim with its forked tongue.

a mispris'd mood What you have mistaken for my anger.

get therefore Get for it.

So sorrow's heaviness . . . stay My sorrow is the heavier for loss of sleep, which now an opportunity offers for me to make up.

tender An offer (of part payment) made by a bankrupt; 'his' is the obsolete genitive of the pronoun 'it' in the previous line.

misprision Mistake. Cf. the verb in line 74.

Then fate o'er-rules . . . oath A meaningless piece of moralizing, quite inappropriate to Puck, which any sensible producer would cut, or give to the more philosophical Oberon.

confounding Breaking.

cheer Countenance.

that costs the fresh blood dear It was a contemporary superstition that with every sigh a drop of blood was lost.

illusion Trick.

Tartar i.e. the Parthians, celebrated as mounted archers.

Hit with Cupid's archery See II, 1, 166.

apple of his eye i.e. the pupil, once thought to be solid and round.

remedy Relief (by returning his love).

mistook by me Mistaken for Demetrius.

fee Payment (in kisses).

fond pageant Foolish exhibition (of themselves).

prepost'rously i.e. the wrong way round. Formed from Latin *prae*, before and *post*, after.

vows so born . . . appears i.e. vows uttered with tears are truthful ones. The chop-logic in much of the dialogue in this scene does not matter in view of the passionate nature of its utterance.

the badge of faith i.e. tears.

advance Increase.

When truth kills truth i.e. when your vows to me cancel your vows to Hermia.

O devilish-holy fray i.e. a fight in which truth is both victor and vanquished (*oxymoron*).

nothing i.e. no difference in the balance between the two, and nought when added together. This idea is repeated in the following two lines.

two scales i.e. the two pans in a balance.

as light as tales As empty as idle gossip.

he loves not you The next line dramatically turns this statement into dramatic irony.

O Helen . . . divine Of the three operated on by the juice Demetrius is the most extravagant in his worship. Such language underlines the artificial nature of this induced love.

Taurus A lofty mountain range in South-east Asia Minor.

crow i.e. black in comparison (another convenient rhyming word).

seal of bliss i.e. the hand by which she can pledge faith to a lover.

O spite! O hell! It is now the more placid Helena who is driven to desperate utterance.

join in souls Agree in spirit.

A trim exploit A fine thing to do. In the same sarcastic mood as Hermia's 'brave touch'.

extort Wrest from her.

but as guest-wise sojourned Went to stay on the temporary basis of a visitor.

Disparage not the faith . . . know Do not treat scornfully a loyalty (mine) of which you are incapable.

aby Pay for.

to thy sound Where I heard your voice coming from.

engilds Brightens up. An artificial creation (from 'gild'; cover with gold).

Yon . . .oes and eyes of light Circles and points of light i.e. the stars; 'yon' indicates the sky.

as you think i.e. your real thoughts.

in spite of To spite.

hasty-footed i.e. passing too quickly (and bringing the moment of separation nearer).

artificial gods Gods creating by their art.

in one key At the same musical pitch.

incorporate Belonging to the same body.

an union in partition Both united and separated. This sentiment oddly echoes that of Lysander in II, 2, 46–9.

Due but to one Heraldic expression describing two coats of arms with one crest.

rent Rend, tear.

Persever The earlier form of 'persevere'.

counterfeit sad looks Assume a sad expression.

Make mouths upon Make faces at.

well carried If successful.

argument Subject for your jests.

Ethiope Ethiopian or Abyssinian. Hermia is a brunette, Helena a blonde.

Seem to break loose Hermia is clinging desperately to Lysander.

Hang off Stop hanging on to me.

burr Prickly head of the burdock, which clings to one's clothing.

like a serpent An ironic parallel to Hermia's dream (II, 2, 145).

bond . . . bond Pun on (a) a signed contract and (b) a fetter.

Since night Since nightfall.

In earnest, shall I say? She is beginning to accept that Lysander has
  changed.

be out of hope . . . doubt i.e. abandon hope, cease to question,
  entertain no doubts.

canker-blossom Worm in the bud.

counterfeit i.e. false image of what I once thought true.

puppet Doll.

prevail'd with Conquered.

painted maypole i.e. thin and tall, with (artificial) colour in her cheeks.
  Perhaps the dark-haired Hermia has a pale complexion.

curst Shrewish.

right maid Really timid woman.

evermore Always (in the past).

stealth Coming secretly.

minimus Tiny creature (Lat. *minimus*, smallest).

knot-grass A common weed, an infusion of which was supposed to
  hinder growth in children and animals.

long of Owing to.

still thou mistak'st i.e. you have blundered again (see line 88).

sort Fall out.

welkin Sky.

drooping Hanging down (to ground level).

Acheron One of four rivers of the classical Hell (a dark place).

testy Quarrelsome.

like Demetrius i.e. to Lysander.

batty wings The flight of the bat is associated with night.

this herb Not 'love-in-idleness', but its antidote, 'Dian's bud'.

virtuous property i.e. power for good.

his might Its magic influence.

derision Mockery. Helena's word, as overheard by Oberon (line 159).

fruitless i.e. with no bad effects.

wend Go. The original present tense of 'went'.

league whose date . . . end Lovers' troth lasting for a life-time.

From monster's view From its attraction to Bottom.

night's swift dragons cut the clouds The chariot of the goddess of
  Night (traditionally drawn by dragons) is passing swiftly through the
  clouds.

fast This rhyming word is tautological.

Aurora's harbinger The Morning Star, fore-runner of Aurora goddess of the dawn. The original 'harbinger' was sent in advance to prepare for the arrival of troops.

Damned spirits . . . night Criminals and suicides were buried at crossroads; as they and the drowned had not received consecrated burial, their spirits were believed to be doomed to wander for a period after death between the hours of midnight and cock-crow.

the Morning's love i.e. Cephalus, who was fond of hunting; he was wooed by Aurora, but remained faithful to his wife Procris.

Neptune i.e. the sea.

streams Used of sea-currents, like the Gulf Stream.

haste, make no delay While urging haste, both Oberon and Puck have been wasting time on some indifferent poetry; however, some minutes had to elapse before the re-entry of the rivals, exhausted in their search for each other.

drawn i.e. with sword in hand.

plainer More level.

Ho, ho, ho! Puck's traditional cry.

spite Annoyance, at either (a) Demetrius hiding from him, or (b) the darknesss thwarting him.

Abide Wait for.

look to be visited i.e. expect me to come and fight you.

Abate Shorten.

Shine, comforts, from the east i.e. let the comforting light of day appear.

sleep, that sometimes shuts up sorrow's eye Cf. the similar personification in line 85.

Steal me awhile from mine own company i.e. let me lose myself in sleep.

Heavens shield Lysander Her love remains true.

When thou wak'st Puck has waited for the arrival of Hermia.

The man shall have his mare again Proverbial.

Revision questions on Act III

1 Explain all the misfortunes which overtake the rehearsal of *Pyramus and Thisbe*.

2 Give a consecutive account of all Puck's activities in this Act.

3 Trace the course of the quarrel between Hermia and Helena.

4 Compare, from the point of view of their comic effect, the spell cast on the two Athenians and Bottom's transformation.

5 What contrasts are noticeable in Act III?

Act IV Scene 1

This time the four lovers sleep soundly while the fairy plot is disentangled. Oberon watches pityingly his queen lavishing attention on Bottom, whose coarse tastes contrast with the dainty suggestions of his fairy lover. His ass's head surprises him only by a novel tickling sensation and the obvious need of a visit to the barber. His ear for music is the same, but his taste for food is now a donkey's. Like the other mortals, he is tired by the long night and lies down to sleep. When Titania follows suit, Oberon, explaining to Puck how he has easily secured his page, anoints her eyes with the antidote and wakens her. Puck then removes the ass's head from Bottom, and the fairies dance to music that deepens the slumbers of the five mortals now lying on the ground. As they depart on their errand, now a joint one, of blessing the palace of Theseus and his bride, hunting horns are heard bringing in the Duke and his train. The royal hunters are discussing the points of their favourite breeds of hound, when they see four of the sleepers (the pleasure of seeing Bottom return to consciousness is reserved for a later occasion!). As the lovers spring up in confusion and amazement, Lysander's defence and Egeus's accusation are followed by Demetrius's announcement of his change of heart, though he cannot explain it.

Theseus thereupon overrules Egeus; he abandons the hunt in order to prepare for a triple wedding, and the royal party leaves the lovers to exclaim in astonishment at what now seems a dream. As soon as they have followed the Duke, Bottom awakes, looks round for his fellow-players and, full of wonder at his own dream, marches off with the idea of adding one more alteration, in his favour, to the play.

Commentary

This scene must constitute a record for the number of characters awaking from sleep! Titania is puzzled to see so many mortals, the mortals at being reconciled, Bottom to find himself alone. Two permanent effects that do not vanish with the dream are the restoration of Demetrius to Helena and the surrender by Titania of her Indian boy to Oberon – though one wonders what kind of explanation she is going to get to her request, 'Tell me how it came this night/That I sleeping here was found'.

Bottom escapes notice by Theseus and the lovers; it is with unconscious irony that during the performance in Act V the Duke jokingly suggests that with the help of a surgeon the half-dead Pyramus might yet recover and 'prove an ass'.

amiable Lovable.

coy Caress.

Mounsieur As 'monsieur' was and is still essential to French polite conversation, this is a ceremonious touch by Bottom.

bring me the honey-bag As suggested by Titania in III, 1, 161.

overflowen with Smothered by an overflow from.

neaf Fist.

leave your courtesy Stop bowing to me.

Cavalery A colloquial English rendering of the Spanish 'caballero', gentleman, cavalier. It alliterates with Cobweb, as Mounsieur does with Mustard-seed. There is a slip here by Bottom or the dramatist, for Pease-blossom, not Cobweb, has been commissioned to scratch.

tongs Struck with a key, as with the triangle.

bottle Small bundle.

exposition of He means 'disposition to'.

all ways In all directions.

woodbine As this is usually Shakespeare's name for the honeysuckle, here it is probably a printer's mistake for 'bindweed' (convolvulus).

the female ivy In classical poetry the vine was 'married' to the elm. Here the idea is applied to the ivy, possibly as more appropriate to a northern climate, and is further developed in the expression 'Enrings the barky fingers', i.e. clings like the ring on the finger of a betrothed person.

dotage Excessive fondness (not, as now, the feebleness of old age).

of late Very recently.

favours Gifts, love-tokens (this time, of flowers).

rounded Girdled.

orient Shining. The earliest precious stones came from the east.

imperfection i.e. the illusion caused by the magic juice.

take the transformed scalp . . . head Taken literally, this expression would mean 'restore Bottom to his human shape by taking off his head!' The dramatic illusion, including Bottom's beautiful dream, may be shattered by its removal on stage, but the audience accepts the stage property with as much delight as it does later the face in the lion's skin and the waving of Moonshine's lantern.

the other i.e. the lovers still asleep on the stage. The Old English plural was 'othre'.

Dian's bud Probably a bud of *Agnus castus*, a tree reputed to inspire chastity.

strike more dead . . . sense i.e. deaden their senses more than in ordinary sleep (so that they shall not be wakened when the fairies 'rock the ground' in the dance which now follows).

new in amity Friends once more.

solemnly With full ceremonial: the same meaning as in 'triumph', a solemn procession. Cf. Theseus' promise to his bride in I, 1, 19.

in silence sad In solemn silence.

night's Pronounced 'nightes', the old genitive form.

observation Observance, as in I, 1, 167. Theseus uses the verb in line 131. The 'rite of May' indicates that the four days have mysteriously elapsed. Cf. line 134.

vaward Vanguard, forepart.

in conjunction i.e. the sound and the echo will clash and produce a mingled noise.

Hercules One of this great hero's twelve labours was to capture a mad bull in Crete. The bear, of which there is no extant record, may be a misprint for 'boar'. Hercules had to deal with a boar that ravaged southern Greece.

Cadmus Brother of Europa, he was the founder of Thebes and sower of the fabulous dragon's teeth.

Crete The island south-east of Greece.

bay'd the bear Brought the bear to 'bay' i.e. to turn and face the dogs which 'bayed'.

Sparta City state in south-east Peloponnesus, famous, among other things, for its dogs.

fountains Springs. Probably a misprint for 'mountains'.

so flew'd, so sanded Having the same flews (overhanging lip of the upper jaw) and the same sandy colour.

dew lapp'd Having loose skin hanging from their throats.

Thessalian bulls Hunting bulls on horseback was a national custom of the men of Thessaly, an ancient kingdom to the north of Greece proper. They were among the first to tame horses, so perhaps originating the belief in 'centaurs' – half men and half horses.

Each under each Rising in a scale. Hounds were chosen to form a pack with barks of different pitches.

Crete . . . Sparta . . . Thessaly Three widely separated places in ancient Greece.

soft An exclamation of warning, common in Shakespeare's day.

wonder of Wonder at.

The rite of May The title of the play is connected with the *idea* of midsummer madness, not with the time of its action.

in grace of our solemnity In honour of our ceremony.

our intent Possibly this means to hunt in the morning, before their wedding.

Saint Valentine i.e. St Valentine's Day (February 14th) on which birds were supposed to choose their mates.

wood-birds Not a species! The pairs of lovers have come together in their surprise.

where we might Whenever we were able to get to.

Enough, enough . . . enough Cf. the old man's captious repetition of 'thou' in I, 1, 28.

I beg the law Any 'schooling' by Theseus has had no effect on this 'Shylock'!

this food A questionable metaphor for a loved one, as artificial as Lysander's 'loathed medicine', III, 2, 264.

natural taste Normal appetite.

overbear Over-rule.

These things i.e. the events in the wood.

undistinguishable Blurred.

parted eye i.e. eyes out of focus.

Mine and not mine own Helena is still unsure of Demetrius, like the finder of a jewel who may have to surrender it to its original owner. He had been out of love with her far longer than Lysander had been with Hermia.

When my cue comes, call me But a cue should be followed without a call; and it was 'never tire'. Bottom has been true to his normal self throughout!

man is but an ass A fine piece of dramatic irony.

patch'd fool Clown (cf. III, 2, 9); but such a 'fool' was rarely at a loss for a word!

a ballad The popular way to commemorate a dramatic episode, as here, or of publishing a scandal, as when Falstaff exclaims, 'And I have not ballads made on you all, and sung to filthy tunes, let a cup of sack be my poison' (*1 Henry V*, II, 2, 43–5). Shakespeare is said to have pinned a ballad on the gate of Sir Thomas Lucy's deer-park at Charlecote, which began:

A parliament member, a justice of peace,
At home a poor scare-crow, at London an ass.

no bottom No fundamental explanation (cf. 'get to the bottom of'); it would thus be a case of Hamlet without the Prince!

her death i.e. Thisbe's death. He forgets that it was to be preceded by his own!

Act IV Scene 2

The actors are bewailing the collapse of their undertaking, which would have made their fortunes, through the spiriting away of Bottom, when he himself bursts in on them to warn them to get ready for the performance, manfully (or in his uncertainty) withholding the story of his experiences until later.

Commentary

This short scene serves the useful purpose of covering the time needed for the characters in the main plot to return to Athens and prepares the audience for the appearance of the play after all.

In the following Act it will not escape notice that the play which was not 'going forward' is suddenly produced with a new title and fresh dialogue, mastered in the interval between Bottom's return and their arrival at the palace!

transported i.e. carried away by fairies.

paramour ... paragon Lover ... model of excellence. It is Quince who here stands corrected.

of naught Worthless.

sixpence a day Worth much more in Elizabethan times, this was an enviable daily allowance.

courageous He means 'glorious', on the analogy of the two meanings of 'brave'.

I am to discourse wonders I have wonderful things to talk about.

I will tell you everything Is the emphasis on 'will' postponing the story to another time (when he will have remembered more), or is he tantalizing his hearers?

strings i.e. to tie them on with.

presently Immediately.

preferred Put on the list of entertainments (from which items would be selected for performance).

Revision questions on Act IV

1 Compare the reactions on awaking, of Titania, Demetrius and Bottom.

2 In what ways are the approach and the actual moment of dawn indicated? How does it influence the action?

3 Make a list of complimentary and uncomplimentary remarks in this Act.

4 How many different kinds of music are mentioned?

5 What three wishes are satisfied during the course of Act IV?

Act V Scene 1

In the final Act, all three groups of characters are brought together in the same building into direct contact with the wedding, now in the foreground: the lovers' reunion makes it a triple wedding; the mechanicals provide visible entertainment; the fairies bestow an invisible blessing.

Theseus, in a highly poetical condemnation of poets and other imaginative people, declares his disbelief in the lovers' account of the events in the wood – which, for her part, Hippolyta is inclined to accept. Upon the arrival of the other two newly wedded couples Theseus calls on Philostrate for the list of the night's entertainments.

The fourth on the list catches his attention by its contradictory title. When the master of the revels explains that it is as 'tedious' as it is 'brief', and that its tragical qualities arouse only 'the passion of loud laughter', Theseus asks about the performers and is told that uneducated workmen have laboured hard to produce it for the occasion. He thereupon selects it for performance, in spite of protests from Philostrate and from Hippolyta too, justifying his choice by indicating the same simple loyalty behind it that he had observed in the almost inarticulate, though carefully rehearsed, speeches of welcome made to him on his visits to other towns.

Philostrate returns, there is a flourish of trumpets, and Quince mispunctuates his way through the first part of the prologue, expressing the exact opposite of what the words are intended to say. The crude efforts of the players are thenceforth the butt of the courtiers' wit, in which Theseus plays a leading, though good-humoured, part. He follows the incidents closely, maintaining a fine balance between his sense of the play's 'palpable grossness' and a real or assumed interest in its development. To his practical mind the best of these dramatic performances is unreal anyway, and this piece, with all its imperfections, has passed the time very pleasantly.

Pyramus and Thisbe

The actors are first paraded before the audience, and the plot and their part in it explained, so that nothing of the ensuing scenes will puzzle the beholders. The cast is as follows:

Prologue	Peter Quince, a carpenter
Pyramus	Nick Bottom, a weaver
Thisbe	Francis Flute, a bellows-mender

Wall	Tom Snout, a tinker
Moonshine	Robin Starveling, a tailor
Lion	Snug, a joiner

Wall introduces himself and his 'cranny'. Pyramus upbraids the black night for the absence of his beloved, and curses the wall for her non-appearance. Thisbe, however, soon enters, and a tender duologue takes place through the cranny. After arranging to meet at Ninus's tomb, they depart, followed by Wall.

A very discreet Lion reassures the ladies, but his partner Moonshine is less successful in commanding attention, for he is constantly interrupted by critical suggestions that he should (1), wear the Moon's horns on his head; (2) put himself inside his own lantern, with the result that his patience is quickly exhausted and, when at last allowed to speak, he jettisons his lines and gives a laconic account of himself and his properties with the surly bluntness of the honest workman who objects to being trifled with.

Thisbe appears, only to be frightened away by the Lion, who tears her mantle and vanishes. Pyramus's rapturous apostrophe to the Moon is broken off by the sight of Thisbe's blood-stained mantle. After a passionate lament, he draws his sword and kills himself theatrically, the stage echoing with his dying groans. Thisbe returns to find her lover lifeless and, uttering a eulogy of his personal beauty, seizes his sword and stabs herself to a death as vocal as his.

Commentary

This production should be compared with *The Nine Worthies* at the end of *Love's Labour's Lost*, which is similarly defended as an honest endeavour, though more mercilessly baited. Shakespeare's fantastic but highly entertaining comic creation is followed by a rustic dance, the proposed Epilogue being rejected. Would it have rivalled the Prologue in ineptitude? It would anyway have come too soon before Puck's own closing appeal.

When the court has retired, Puck enters by the light of the dying fire to introduce the fairy revels. 'Wasted brands'? Still glowing in the hearth of the moonlit hall, they may seem inappropriate to the month of May: perhaps it has proved chillier, in our changeable climate, than the previous night when there was much slumbering in the wood! Oberon's benediction on the palace and its occupants controverts Theseus's sober address on the poet's falsifying imagination that 'gives to airy nothing/A local habitation and a name.'

The variations in metre are of interest. After the blank verse of the Duke's observations comes Quince's Prologue, composed, presumably by him, in quatrains, with concluding couplets. The first part is the famous contradictory preface, in stanza form, two quatrains and a couplet; the second and longer part, running to three quatrains and a couplet, with one rogue line, followed by two more quatrains and a couplet, correctly punctuated (as if to show that the author is quite capable of this if he likes), introduces the actors personally. The dialogue is similar, with ambitious opening quatrains by hero and heroine and even the Lion. As the climax approaches, passions are worked up into an extreme parody of exclamatory staccato short-lined stanzas, of the sort once memorized by miracle players; everything is apostrophized, from the cruel Fates to the wicked Wall and the death-dealing sword. Meanwhile Theseus and the other two bridegrooms, in relaxed mood, have resorted for the first time to disjointed prose for their running commentary.

After the dance the Duke dismisses the court at the witching hour of midnight in dignified blank verse. Was it his 'imagination' or a last piece of gentle mockery or a mere sense of popular tradition that impels him to add: ''tis almost fairy time'? The rest is lilting trochaic verse: first Puck, with his characteristic evocation of churchyard ghosts, brandishes his broom; next the fairy king and queen lead a more graceful dance than the Bergomask; finally Oberon bids their followers visit every room to bring peace and an untainted issue to every couple (should this task take all night it would at least indicate the size of the palace!).

Puck remains behind to turn and face the real audience which has followed the strange events of the night with unspoken criticism, but some laughter; if they have found the performance slight and unmeritable they can dismiss it as something they have dreamt up in their sleep; if they approve (in the usual fashion) he can promise something still better.

More strange than true Pleased with the outcome (relieving him from having to impose a serious penalty) the sober-minded Theseus dismisses the explanation of its working out. In the light of what has taken place in full view of the audience, this practical disbeliever in dreams now utters a lengthy piece of dramatic irony.

may Can.

antique fables Strange stories.

fairy toys Fairy-tales.

seething Literally, boiling. Cf. the past participle in 'drink-sodden'.

shaping fantasies Imaginations that create non-existent forms.

of imagination all compact Made entirely of imagination, i.e. it dominates their thinking. Now the 'poet' has been added to form a trio, afflicted each by a specific form of 'frenzy', Theseus's diatribe is involuntarily 'transformed' into an often-quoted paean of praise of the poetic imagination. The last five lines are a relapse into the prosaic utterance, sympathetic but uninspired, of this quite English nobleman.

Helen's beauty in a brow of Egypt The beauty of Helen of Troy in a dark-faced gypsy. No reference here to blonde Helen and brunette Hermia, just the Duke's lofty generalization of the popular preference. Nedar's daughter, whose sad story had slipped his mind in I, 1, 114, is now simply one of a quartette whose differences have been conveniently settled 'out of court'. And the two former rivals now sit demurely through the entertainment, leaving all comment to their respective betrothed.

if it would but apprehend . . . that joy It (imagination) has only to think of happiness and straightaway it finds some cause for this happiness. Such is Theseus' commonsense explanation of the night's happenings – the lovers, having solved their love problem among themselves, have thought up a miracle to account for it. The repetition of 'apprehend' and 'comprehend' together (cf. lines 5–6) would indicate that these inferior five lines are later padding. The student should consult a dictionary to 'comprehend' the confusion that has arisen over their use.

some fear Something to be afraid of.

But all the story . . . admirable Theseus's independent-minded bride disagrees: 'But the story as a whole, together with the fact that the minds of all four were similarly affected, proves that it is something more than their imagination and tends to be quite consistent; it is, nevertheless, a strange and marvellous story.'

More than to us More than our share (of joy and love).

after-supper Dessert. While the tables were being cleared after the main course (the action of Fr. 'desservir') various fruits and sweetmeats were consumed.

abridgement Either (a) a shortened performance like an *interlude*, or (b) something to while away the time.

beguile The lazy time Make the slow-moving hours pass more quickly.

brief List. In the Folio Edition, Lysander is given it to read out. This might seem to brand the mighty Theseus as illiterate!

ripe Ready.

'The battle with the Centaurs . . .' Hercules and Theseus were both present at a wedding of the Lapithae, to which the Centaurs had been invited, but the insolent behaviour of the latter led to their expulsion after a hard fight.

'The riot of the tipsy Bacchanals . . .' Orpheus, a legendary pre-Homeric poet and musician, greatly loved his wife Eurydice; when she died he went to Hades to seek her. By playing sweet music he charmed Pluto and persuaded him to let Eurydice go back with him to the world. The god of the underworld made one condition, that Orpheus was not to look back until they were both outside Hades. When Orpheus saw daylight he looked back to see if his wife was following, and immediately she disappeared. His grief for her was so great that the jealous women of Thrace tore him to pieces in one of the wild orgies customary at the feast of Bacchus.

device Entertainment.

from Thebes . . . a conqueror Thebes, an ancient Greek city, and inveterate enemy of Athens, was not conquered by Theseus. Legend speaks only of his helping the sole survivor of an attack on the city to rescue the bodies of the slain.

The thrice three Muses This, the only non-Greek topic, was probably inserted as an allusion to contemporary literary complaints. Note that it is dismissed as satire, unsuitable for a wedding. The Muses, nine in number, were the goddesses who inspired song, poetry and other arts.

sorting with Suited to.

'A tedious brief scene' Altered from 'the most lamentable comedy and most cruel death of Pyramus and Thisbe'.

strange The context would suggest that this is a misprint in the early editions for some epithet of blackness. Perhaps snow followed ice and, being only too familiar and nothing to be wondered at, was given an epithet as incongruous as 'hot' is for ice.

the concord of this discord i.e. the meaning of this contradiction.

fitted Fitting his role.

toil'd their unbreath'd memories Exercised their untrained memories.

intents Efforts at performance.

stretch'd Extending beyond their powers.

conn'd Learned.

When simpleness and duty tender it When dutifully offered by simple men. The *personification* is continued by Hippolyta with 'wretchedness' and 'duty'.

take what they mistake Understand what they fail to express adequately.

what poor duty . . . merit When the dutiful offer their poor best, the courtesy of a generous mind will applaud them for what they are able to do and not criticize them for their faults. This ideal of polite attention, however, is – in the interests of comedy – scarcely attained in what follows.

Where I have come . . . In her royal progresses Elizabeth was greeted with elaborate speeches of welcome.

clerks Scholars.

premeditated Prepared.

Make periods in the midst of sentences A classic example is about to be perpetrated by Quince! 'Periods' means full-stops.

Throttle . . . fears Choke down in their fear the words so carefully rehearsed beforehand.

the modesty of fearful duty The bashfulness of those who are scared of paying their respects. Notice the continued personifications.

In least . . . capacity Utter sincerest loyalty in the fewest words, in my opinion.

address'd Ready.

If we offend . . . like to know If properly punctuated, this famous prologue may be taken to run something like this:

'If we offend you, we would have you know that we do not intend to give offence, but honestly to do our humble best. That is the first thing we are aiming at. Think that we come not to spite, but to please you. Our purpose is entirely to afford you pleasure. We are not here to make you sorry for it. Here are our actors and their performance will tell you all there is to know about it.'

stand upon points Bother about punctuation marks.

rid his prologue . . . stop Got through his prologue like a young horse not yet trained to stop.

true Accurately.

recorder A kind of flute.

in government Properly regulated (by his fingers).

nothing impaired i.e. no link missing.

disordered i.e. tangled up.

Lion hight by name Is called a Lion; 'by name' is tautological.

fall Let fall, drop.

with bloody mouth The Prologue, first mooted by Bottom to allay fears in the audience, is given some fearful wording!

sinister Left. This Latin word, which came through superstitious attitudes about the left to mean 'threatening harm', was here probably adopted as a very imperfect rhyme to 'whisper.'

O grim-look'd night! An example of what Shakespeare is parodying is to be found in the early tragedy *Gorboduc*:

Oh, Eubulus, oh, draw this sword of ours,
And pierce this heart with speed! O hateful light!
O loathsome life! O sweet and welcome death!

Jove shield thee Heaven protect thee.

sensible Able to feel.

hair Used with lime in making cement.

think what thou wilt An argumentative expression, out of place here.

thy lover's grace This could be anything from divine favour to physical attraction.

Limander He means 'Leander', who swam the Hellespont to visit Hero.

Helen A blunder for Hero

Shafalus to Procrus Mispronunciations of Cephalus and Procris (see note to III, 2, 389).

'Tide life, 'tide death i.e. whether life or death be the result. The archaic 'betide' (happen) is still used in expressions like 'Woe betide you'.

mure rased The wall is down; 'morall downe', a faulty reading in the Folio has been variously emended: 'mural downe' (Pope), but there is no record of 'mural' as a noun; 'mure rased' (Brooks, see Appendix II, p.159ff. of the Arden edition of the *Dream*) which might well be the mock rendering of the more homespun 'the wall is down'. Perhaps by reason of some allusion hidden from posterity, the word 'wall' has been used over and over again, with unusual emphasis. The word 'rased' would also pin-point the incongruity of this actor-cum-stage-prop merely walking off the stage, like his colleague Moonshine, who departs at the request of the dying hero, leaving Thisbe to find her lover in the starlight.

No remedy . . . warning There is nothing else to do with walls that unexpectedly hear all you say but to pull them down. (Walls have always been suspected of hiding unwanted listeners.)

in this kind i.e. of stage performers.

the worst are no worse i.e. they are the same shadows.

if imagination amend them If the audience's imagination makes up for their defects.

not theirs Hippolyta is more practical if less charitable.

lion fell Lion's skin (and not a fierce lion). This is clear from the next line, '*if* I should as lion come'.

nor else no lion's dam And no lioness either (see *Sources*, para 3).

This lion is a very fox The bravery of the lion and the cunning of the fox were often contrasted. Snug the Lion is said to be as brave as a slinking fox and as discreet as a cackling goose.

leave it to his discretion After trying to follow this exchange of wit, the wise student will think discretion the better part of valour, and listen in his turn to Moonshine!

the horned moon i.e. the crescent.

the horns on his head Once imagined as the mark of a cuckold, a man whose wife had been unfaithful to him, the name being falsely attributed to him from the female cuckoo which lays its eggs in other birds' nests. The cuckoo's two notes were said to be a warning to an unfortunate husband (Cf. note II, 1, 126). This topic has always been good for a joke.

He is no crescent i.e. he is round of face (unlike the moon he is representing) so any horns he may be wearing would be contained within the circle.

the Man i'th'Moon This change of name gives rise to some further wise-cracking, from which he emerges as a crusty farm-hand, engaged in making a hedge of thorns, accompanied by his dog, and irritated at such interruption in his task. Cf. note III, 1, 55.

for the candle Because of the candle.

in snuff A pun on (1) being extinguished, and (2) angry.

change i.e. like the moon, into another phase, e.g. 'in the wane.'

his small light of discretion i.e. the candle is flickering, and the actor's patience is nearly exhausted.

in all reason As reasonable people.

Well shone, Moon This suggests some frantic activity with the lantern.

moused i.e. shaken as a cat shakes a mouse.

dole Sorrow.

Furies The three classical Furies carried out the vengeance of the gods.

Fates The three classical Fates controlled the lives of individual men: one held the distaff of birth, another spun the thread of life, and the third (who was blind) severed it with the scissors of death.

thrum The tufted end of the thread when fastened to the loom (an appropriate figure for a weaver).

Quail Kill (the same as 'quell').

beshrew Devil take. A mild oath, cf. II, 2, 53.

deflower'd Violated.

look'd with cheer Had always a cheerful look.

confound Ruin, put to confusion or, possibly, blur my vision.

Tongue 'Sun' seems the best emendation. A misprint could be made from the contemporary spelling, 'sonne'.

no die, but an ace i.e. not the dice, but the '1' on it.

but one i.e. one death, not five.

an ass Pun on 'ace'. Unknown to Theseus, Bottom has already been one.

How chance How does it happen.

God warrant us God save us (from all such).

God bless us Similarly, God protect us, but used more as an expression of astonishment.

means Printed in Folio and Quarto editions, this dialect word of Old English origin = mourns. It may have been due to association with *videlicet*; namely, or that means: Theobald suggested 'moans'.

O Sisters Three See note line 274.

imbrue Drench (with blood).

the wall is down Bottom has the last word: no family reconciliation as in that other lovers' tragedy *Romeo and Juliet*; Snout, like Starveling and Snug, has simply walked off the stage. And there are no dead for them to bury anyway!

Bergomask Rustic, clownish, from the Italian town of Bergamo. Bottom has interchanged 'hear' and 'see'.

your play needs no excuse i.e. in the traditional form of an epilogue, spoken by one of the actors (cf. the Epilogue to *As You Like It*). In our play it is to be the fairy Puck who defends the whole performance by suggesting that the audience has dreamt it all.

iron tongue Church bell's clapper. Anachronism.

fairy time Dramatic irony. Theseus knows nothing of the fairy revels about to commence.

overwatch'd Kept awake too long.

palpable-gross i.e. of a grossness (or crudity) that can be felt or seen.

heavy gait Slow pace.

behowls Howls at. Cf. note on the intensive prefix 'be–' in I, 1, 131.

fordone Utterly worn out; 'for' is another intensive prefix.

wasted Burnt up.

In remembrance of In mind of.

triple Hecate's team The three-in-one goddess, Diana, of hunting and chastity on earth, Phoebe, of the moon in the heavens, and Hecate, in the underworld, is here riding in her moon-chariot.

behind the door i.e. from where it would have been swept by lazy Athenian (or Elizabethan) servants.

rehearse Repeat.

by rote Memorizing without necessarily understanding.

the issue The only child of Theseus and Hippolyta, named Hippolytus, suffered a violent death.

prodigious Unnatural.

this field-dew consecrate A third magic juice!

take his gait Go his way.

several Individual.

break of day When fairies return to their world.

shadows Puck means his fellow-fairies, whose king is Oberon (III, 2, 347); but one senses an echo of Theseus's earlier comment (line 208): 'The best in this kind are but shadows.'

No more yielding but Producing no more than.

reprehend Find fault with.

the serpent's tongue i.e. the audience's hiss.

make amends i.e. with another play. Elizabethan plays followed each other, with rather short runs.

Give me your hands i.e. clap them.

restore amends One last contrived rhyme which, if it means anything, is tautological.

Revision questions on Act V

1 Give in your own words Theseus's views on (a) poetry, (b) drama, (c) oratory.

2 What features do you notice to be common to the lovers' plot and the artisans' play?

3 Which of the spectators' criticisms have dramatic point, and which are jests at the expense of the actors?

4 Explain the parts played in this scene by (a) Philostrate, (b) Puck.

5 Distinguish the different kinds of verse employed in Act V, and say how they contribute to our appreciation of this long scene.

Shakespeare's art in
A Midsummer Night's Dream

'Thou art not for an age but for all time.' (Ben Jonson)

Introduction

Shakespeare achieved two firsts in our national literature, as poet and as playwright – something not claimed for any man of letters in any other nation. His plays have received worldwide recognition; his poetry is embedded in the dialogue of those plays. His powers of expression matched his genius in the creation of character. His lines, the best of which were poetically inspired, were composed for the utterance of professional actors entertaining audiences of varying tastes. He knew his fellow-actors and the roles they were best at undertaking. Through them as mouthpieces he was also at work on the minds of those who watched his dramas unfold, showing them human nature at its best and its worst, stimulating their imaginations by bringing old stories to life before their eyes and affording them opportunities to exercise their judgement between right and wrong, loyalty and treachery, love and hate, wisdom and folly. They beheld good and evil deeds, understood the motives and flinched at the consequences. All the world became a stage, and for the space of a dream the stage became a world in itself – ideal, not real, the shadow for the substance, a world of tricks and illusions in which a man is so easily supposed an ass. For generations it has been argued that his marvellous inventions could not possibly be the work of a countryman come up to town; the mystery of his personality, on the other hand, reinforces the appeal of his creations.

He was many-sided, with no bias, no doctrine to preach, no malice towards his contemporaries, no subservience to authority and no respect for mobs; he sculpted life from the beautiful to the grotesque, without sentiment or cynicism. What personal feelings he had – attractions to friends and emotional involvements with women – he expressed in a few poems and sonnets which cannot be positively said to be either based on real experience or written merely as literary exercises. In brief, Shakespeare was a poetical dramatist, not a poet who used the forms of drama, as did our second greatest poet, John Milton. It is the poetry that enriches the study of his work away from the stage and endows his characters with the immortality of endless editions.

His greatness was acknowledged in his own day, and his works, while they fluctuated in public esteem during the following centuries, have never been more popular than during the past hundred years. Scholars in various parts of the world have devoted years, in some cases a lifetime, to wider and more intensive research into the texts, and to the discovery of fresh clues and new interpretations. In all but a few of his plays his imagination and wealth of diction have stirred the hearts of full houses – the voices may change, but the words are the same. The Old Vic Theatre took five years to present the entire series. None of his plays was written for the study: all had to come across the boards to that sea of faces on whose reception (handclaps or hisses) depended their success or failure. Least of all would their author have expected to be a staple topic for generations of students taking examinations in English Literature.

In the following commentary opinions are those formed or accepted by the editor; they are offered to the student as an aid to forming his own judgements and, it is hoped, getting more enjoyment from this play. There are, happily, no real villains (rare enough in Shakespeare), only mischief-makers from the fairy world. The prevailing atmosphere is one of enchantment, and the characters mostly wonder what is happening to them, while Theseus, full of wise sayings, has no inkling of what the supernatural gets up to in his absence. The contrast between the visible and the unseen worlds, which has teased so many imaginative minds, could not have been expressed in a more delightful 'fantasy'.

Structure, theme and setting

Structure

The marriage of Theseus is the framework of the play. The opening and closing scenes are set in his palace. The ceremony sets in motion the three plots, one the lovers' quarrel, which must be settled by the wedding-day and may be called the main plot, and the other two running closely parallel to it, but never crossing it – the fairy quarrel and the play production – which, when they join, in the persons of Titania and Bottom, achieve a comic climax which is an admirable foil to the shrill outcries of the bemused lovers.

All the complications are started and worked out in the wood. The entanglements and disentanglements are effected by the juices of two magic flowers, known only to the fairy king. Indeed, Oberon's whims, not human impulses, shape 'the course of true love', in which case the slightest of character delineation is sufficient – no more, let us say, than for the persons of a masque, that typical Elizabethan wedding entertainment. And since a masque must have its anti-masque, the spirit of mischief, embodied in Puck, supplies that element of the grotesque by turning the mimic lover into a real ass, and so separating him, for a time, from his Thisbe more dramatically than any plaster partition or roaring lion's skin.

The human characters pass from the rule of day to the rule of night, and back again. By day, the Athenian duke passes judgement in the light of custom and tradition, by night the 'king of shadows' exercises magic powers in quite arbitrary fashion; the one interprets the law, the other knows no law but his own passing emotions. The lovers flee from submission to an unshakeable law founded on a moral (if narrow) principle, to find themselves subjected to the vagaries of quite non-moral fancies, which afterwards appear to them but the fantasies of a dream. But unreal and transitory as a dream may be, some trace of the shadow-play passes on into the returning day, and Helena regains Demetrius.

The enchanted visions of a midsummer night's dream are thus framed in the sober realities of day. At cock-crow fairies bring their moonlit revels to an end, while the court has already risen to begin a day of festivities by hunting; the blare of horns and the barking of hounds dispel the atmosphere of charm and counter charm, of mocking spirits and bewitched mortals. The roles of actor and spectator shift too from one set of characters to another: while the theatre audience are entertained by the fairy intrigue, the sprites themselves enjoy the scene of confusion among the lovers, who laugh heartily in their turn at a comedy which, some critics say, burlesques the midnight 'Comedy of Errors' in which they have just played their parts. Certainly, in the lovers' plot we see misunderstanding that nearly becomes tragic; and in the artisans' interlude tragedy misunderstood into comedy.

In a play where sudden transformations are the order of the night, where the ass must to the barber's and the lion is a gentle conscientious beast, incongruities need not be dwelt upon. It is sufficient to note in passing the two explanations of the Indian boy's origin (II, 1, 22 and 123); the two versions of *Pyramus and Thisbe*; and the 'abridgements' of time which make it possible for a fifteen-minute play to beguile three hours, and for Theseus's encounter with the lovers to wear away so much of the morning that the hunt is given up. These may be in part due to some rearrangement (and consequent shortening) of the play for an actual wedding performance, though there is no evidence for it. In this connection the title of the play, the events of which belong to the month of May, may indicate either a first performance in midsummer (cf. *Twelfth Night*) or that spirit of revelry and spell-binding that formerly characterized the summer solstice.

The detection of loose ends should never detract from our admiration for Shakespeare's dramatic construction, especially in two respects: (1) the combination of two or more plots into one harmonious whole, with little regard for the 'classical unities' of *time* (twenty-four hours), *place* (one neighbourhood) and *action* (one main plot only), thus reflecting the complexities of his and our day; (2) the blending of the two distinct dramatic forms of tragedy and comedy as a mirror to the mixture of tears and laughter that is still the lot of most individuals. Tragedy was unavoidable in the Histories with their reversals of fortune, but into his tragedies he introduced 'comic relief' and in his comedies he allowed events to take a temporarily serious turn. Was he indulging in self-mockery when he parodied this tendency to mix the funny with the painful in *Pyramus and Thisbe*, or did he simply recollect its brash appearance on the title-page of a less successful play, Preston's *Cambyses* (1570) sub-titled 'a lamentable tragedy mixed full of pleasant mirth'?

One wonders what Shakespeare would think were he to be present at the performance of one of those 'fringe' productions that have strained the structure of his plays to the utmost, not to mention inexcusably mutilated the dialogue. Would he wake 'amazedly' as from some nightmare?

Theme

In *A Midsummer Night's Dream* love is represented in many variations, from fairy spells to wedding festivities. Unlike some modern comedies, the complications of Shakespeare's lovers are resolved in their wedding; the ceremony marks the happy ending. It has a part too in the action of a number of plays. There is the mock wedding in *As You Like It*, when Orlando pretends to take the hand of his love Rosalind, quite deceived by her disguise as a shepherd boy; the wedding of mistaken identity in *Twelfth Night*, whereby Olivia is contracted to a complete stranger, having taken him for the page (his twin sister in disguise) whom she has until then wooed in vain. Then there is the interrupted wedding of Hero in *Much Ado About Nothing*, broken off through the false slander of a villain; the placing by Portia in *The Merchant of Venice* of a ring on her husband's finger, only to win it back again as a reward for saving his friend's life in court, while disguised as a judge.

In our play the wedding is the basis of the entire fabric. It attracts the fairies, whose spells save Hermia from a nunnery and restore Demetrius to Helena. It leads Bottom to rehearse in a wood and he finds himself right in the middle of fairyland. The opposite of a wedding, 'single blessedness', is presented in two very different lights: Theseus warns Hermia that 'the livery of a nun' is something to be 'endured' (I, 1, 70); on the other hand, Oberon describes to Puck how the arrow from Cupid's bow passed harmlessly by the 'imperial votress' of Diana, leaving her 'In maiden meditation, fancy-free' (II, 1, 164).

Of love itself we may distinguish three kinds: (1) the passionate, headstrong love of youth; (2) the mature love of older people with responsibilities, in whom passion is subordinated to duty; and (3) the ephemeral love of the fairies with their petty quarrels and reconciliations.

1 By the lovers we are shown first the trials of true love thwarted by a parent, leading to open rebellion and an elopement, and then, at different points in the play, the envy of another's charms, the dog-like devotion of the rejected, hatred for the once loved, and jealousy towards one who has become a successful lover. The mystery of infatuation, which brings about seemingly unaccountable changes of affection is, in a manner, symbolized by the workings of the love-juice, which affects the eyes only (cf. Helena's soliloquy, I, 1, 234).

2 With Theseus and Hippolyta, the tale of their past loves is over, and it is time to settle down to the solid enjoyment of social festivities and field sports.

3 Oberon calmly perverts the love of his own queen out of spite, because she will not satisfy his whim. Having seen Lysander suddenly amorous of Helena, we are prepared for the still stranger attachment of Titania to Bottom; she seeks to make him an 'airy spirit' like herself, apparently by fond embraces.

Setting

The great majority of Shakespeare's scenes (apart from those in the Histories) are set in places abroad, a device which of itself gave them a romantic colouring in the minds of a largely untravelled audience. Only a few privileged individuals could know what Verona, Illyria and Venice were really like, so that the incongruity of English 'local colour' would pass largely unnoticed. Similarly, in plays where the action takes place in Ancient Rome and Athens, those details which are wrong because they belong to a much later period, and which are called anachronisms, would not strike a false note in an age more familiar with classical stories than with their setting.

There is little, therefore, to distinguish Theseus in his palace from any English earl in his castle, or the Athenian craftsmen from their counterparts in the small town or village adjoining the castle. The bones of ancient Greece are clothed in Warwickshire flesh and blood, the fellow townsmen of Shakespeare's youth.

In *A Midsummer Night's Dream*, indeed, there is rather more of the nominal setting and rather less of contemporary life and manners than is usual in his comedies, the chief reasons being (1) that he makes a liberal use of classical mythology drawn from his reading, particularly the translation of Ovid, and (2) the bulk of the action, located in a wood, leaves small scope for the references to 16th-century customs, fashions and sports that spring so naturally to the lips of characters in his other comedies.

Apart from the law that gave authority to a parent to marry off his child as he pleased, the Athenian background is composed wholly of classical myth and legend: the triple goddess Diana (chastity and hunting)/Phoebe (the moon)/Hecate (the underworld); the winged Cupid and Venus's doves; Apollo's pursuit of Daphne; Aurora's wooing of Cephalus, who remained faithful to his wife Procris (Chute's *Cephalus and Procris* appeared in 1593). Also the beauty of Helen of Troy; the despair of Dido, Queen of Carthage, at the departure of the 'false Trojan' Aeneas, to found Rome; the pastoral flirtations of Corin and Phillida; the blackness of the River Acheron and the whiteness of the summit of Mount Taurus; the fabulous Centaurs; the prowess of Hercules; and the fame of Spartan hounds and Thessalian bulls.

It must be admitted, however, that these shadows of antiquity belong more to the sphere of literary allusion than to stage realism; there would be more significance to Shakespeare's patrons in such matters as the nine-men's morris, the maze-tracks on the village green, the churchway path, the spicy 'gossip's bowl', the churning of butter, heraldic coats of arms, painted maypoles, topical ballads (IV, 1, 213), the superstition of St Valentine's Day and – the most conspicuous anachronism in the play – jackdaws 'cawing at the gun's report'. Even these comparatively few features of Shakespeare's own day (mostly mentioned by the fairies) contribute far less of local colour – necessary in a drama so dependent on word-painting to clothe the bare boards of its stage – than do the glimpses of an English woodland, teeming with wild life and haunted by elves. We hear of, though we do not see, the snake's 'enamell'd skin', the bat's 'leathern wings', the fiery glow-worm and the 'painted' butterfly, the briars and thorns that snatch at one's apparel, the adder with its 'double tongue', the hooting owl and 'thorny' hedgehog, the squirrel's hoard and the humble-bee's honey-bag, nodding violets and sweet musk roses, the twisting woodbine's canopy and beds of 'faint' primroses, and that host of smaller creatures against which the tiny fairies must defend themselves.

These fairies, never seen by mortals, though still believed in by many of Shakespeare's spectators, are given both 'local habitation and a name' in what is almost certainly their first play on the English stage. The association of these sprites of Teutonic origin with figures of classical antiquity is itself an anachronism co-extensive with the play, and possible only in Romantic drama. They meet and associate in a moonlit dreamland, where time is meaningless and distance is annihilated. There is no point, therefore, in drawing attention to discrepancies between the ancient worship of the chaste Diana and the Rite of May, an early pagan observance converted into a Christian festival, with overnight preparations and daylight revels.

The Rite of May This was the first of three main festivals in the calendar, the others being Midsummer and Christmas. Long before the dawn of May 1st young people used to go to the woods in search of green boughs for the decoration of houses, and flowers for the May Queen. Daylight games and 'triumphs' (of the kind briefly referred to by Theseus) followed her coronation. There was dancing round the maypole, a very tall post painted in two colours spirally (III, 2, 296). This celebration of the end of winter would be inappropriate in Greece as late as May, but it provides Theseus with an explanation for two pairs of lovers foot-loose in the forest overnight. On any other day they might have been suspect. The horns blown to waken the lovers were a feature of May Day. Once the Queen was not alone; she had a May Lord: formerly responsible for some of the wilder pastimes, he did not survive Puritan reforms. The word 'lord' is used in the play, but sparingly and not in this connection. It was not unusual for lovers to wait superstitiously for the new moon before marriage, but for some reason May was avoided.

Moonlight The moonbeams which inspire in different ways 'The lunatic, the lover and the poet' are the dramatist's creation, drawing, as we have seen, on native and foreign material. By the power of his imagination magic by moonlight casts its spell over the audience in the broadest of daylight. Incidentally, the word 'lunatic' (from Latin *luna*, the moon) then meant a crazy person, temporarily driven out of his mind, as well as what we understand by 'certified inmate'. Phoebe was worshipped each month at the new or the full moon; she was imagined as being driven across the night sky in a chariot pulled by horses or even cows (hence perhaps the horns), but in this play the only reference is to the chariot of Hecate (Underworld) in V, 1, 370. The chastity imposed on her followers by Diana, the third person in this pagan trinity, is represented by the life of a priestess made the alternative to death as the penalty for filial disobedience. From this danger Hermia flees to the wood with her Lysander, followed by Demetrius, followed in turn by Helena. In this moonlit world the fairies rule: the affections of the two men are successively switched from Hermia to Helena by anointing with potent juice – something that would not happen in the city; the rivals are separated by instant fog conjured up by Puck. The comic counterpart to these passionate encounters is the infatuation of Titania for the ass's head placed on Bottom's shoulders, a transformation that, again, could not have taken place at Quince's house. The setting is moonlight, the agents are the fairies, by magic Helena becomes the adored, Hermia the despised.

The moon itself (rather than herself) is remote and chaste; to Theseus cold and fruitless; to Oberon watery enough to quench Cupid's flaming dart; to Titania a moist planetary influence over the seasons; to the mechanicals the traditional Man in the Moon, whose lantern represents stage illumination before the time of floodlights.

Music and Masque The enchantment finds musical expression in the songs and dances of the fairies, which have since been given a setting in the graceful compositions of Mendelssohn. Music, special stage effects and highly poetical speeches uttered by mythical characters made up the masques privately performed in the houses and grounds of Elizabethan noblemen. While

Shakespeare introduces masque-like scenes into several of his plays, this play as a whole is his closest approach to this allegorical form of entertainment. Its performance gains substantially from a full musical accompaniment and elaborate dances; it finds an ideal setting in a garden shrubbery. Shakespeare himself may have looked on, as a boy of eleven, at a spectactular production at Kenilworth Castle, a few miles from his home. These masques would contain veiled, often scandalous allusions to prominent people, including the aristocracy, at times even Royalty. In fact a prominent feature of the masque was its being a 'topical hit'.

Anti-masque Another feature, the anti-masque, or grotesque foil to the graceful evolutions of the masque proper (often in the form of rustics, wild creatures or uncouth monsters) finds a parallel in *Pyramus and Thisbe*, followed by its Bergomask dance. But there is a more definite purpose to be seen in the way this interlude parodies two things: (1) the crude play-acting in local village pageants, in which the actors would be solemnly paraded, any misunderstanding by the audience of their efforts obviated by an explanatory prologue, and the whole effect made more humorous than impressive by the amateurish use of stage 'props'; (2) the ranting dialogue of such earlier forms of drama as the morality plays of the guilds in towns like Coventry (also not far from Stratford), still being performed in Shakespeare's early days.

Contemporary references The Elizabethan preference of blondes to brunettes (Queen Elizabeth I had sandy-coloured hair) would give emphasis to Lysander's vituperation of Hermia – 'Ethiope', 'tawny Tartar' – and to Theseus's sketch of the imaginative lover who can see beauty in a 'brow of Egypt'. Theseus's reference to great clerks who had purposed 'to greet him with premeditated welcomes' would bring to the minds of the audience the addresses of welcome to Elizabeth I on her royal progresses.

Such topical references were a source of interest when humorous journals, gossip columns and cartoons were yet unthought of. The stage was, indeed, a platform for opinions of all kinds, though far less of this (and much of it doubtful) is to be found in Shakespeare than in some of his fellow-playwrights, and there is usually a genial touch in Shakespeare. The idea that ladies would be frightened by a lion may be one such playful allusion to a particular incident (see 'you would frighten the duchess and the ladies', I, 2), but it is more likely to have become a stock joke. Actors are known to have received pensions from Elizabeth when she was pleased with their performances, and perhaps Flute's belief that Bottom 'could not have 'scaped sixpence-a-day' was one of a number of hints that largesse to players was a necessary attribute of sovereigns.

Conservation footnote In 1756 the vicar who owned New Place in Stratford-upon-Avon cut down the mulberry tree, said to have been planted by Shakespeare, to save himself the trouble of showing it to visitors. Soon after this the irascible clergyman had the whole house levelled and left the town, cursed by its inhabitants. In 1769 the actor, David Garrick, played a leading part in establishing the cult of the poet and was presented with the freedom of the town in a basket made of mulberry wood. Today there is a mulberry in the garden believed to be from a cutting of the original.

The characters

Bottom

If I do it, let the audience look to their eyes.

While the fantastic, dream-like incidents of this play call for little depth of character, it is to be noticed that the three persons possessing more individuality than the others are precisely those who assert their authority in their respective and widely differing spheres. Theseus, a born ruler of men, administers justice according to the law, with practical sagacity and gentle tact; Oberon, gifted with supernatural powers, gratifies his own whims, at one moment malicious, at the next benevolent; Bottom seizes power over his neighbours in the same street by sheer force of personality. The first, as it were, holds the ring, doing little, but passing shrewd comment on the world as he sees it; the second actively controls the movements of those who come within the bounds of his magic spells; the last thrusts himself right into the centre of things, sublimely unaware of the figure he cuts, dominating in turn the rehearsal, the fairy court and, during the entertainment, the duke's palace itself. If not the central character of the play, his bulk in it is such that without him the play would be 'marred'; he is, indeed, the first of that great band of comic characters whose vein of humour, conscious and unconscious, is the salt of so many of Shakespeare's plays.

He is, perhaps, the dramatist's fullest portrait of the Elizabethan tradesman; beside him, Dogberry in *Much Ado About Nothing*, and the Cobbler in *Julius Caesar*, are but sketches. His ambition is consuming; his constant desire is to *be somebody*, even several people at once. No part is beyond his powers; his gifts will grace any occasion; he is never at a loss for a word; his explanations and advice, his discovery of difficulties, and the devices he has already thought of to solve them, are all indispensable to the success of whatever is being undertaken. He is free from embarrassment, whether by the sudden inexplicable desertion by his comrades or by the wheedling flatteries of Titania; his wit, his voice, and his person are praised to his face by her, and in his absence by them, but in these respects, however, he has a more becoming sense of his limitations; wit enough to get out of the wood is sufficient for him, and however enthralled Titania may be, his 'honest neighbours' have lost their regard for him, and left him in the lurch.

Like Helena, he feels he is the victim of a conspiracy to mock him, to make a terrified 'ass' of him, and most delicious of dramatic irony, it is his actual transformation into an ass that is the cause of their apparent 'knavery'. It is the characteristic of asses to be unconscious of their affliction, and Bottom enters with his long ears and twitching scalp into the experiences of his dream, determined to acquit himself as lord of the fairies as thoroughly as he can discharge the part of a lover or a tyrant. He is the only one of the mortals to see the fairies (but not with his normal vision) and he accepts them and their services with the same stolid satisfaction as he accepts the hero's role. He addresses them in turn in that tone of pompous familiarity with which he is accustomed to form acquaintances among the citizens of his own quarter of Athens.

Bottom is not all egotist; there is a selflessness about his enthusiasm for the interlude, in spite of his instinctive desire to monopolize the acting and to mould the production after his own ideas. When he wakes from his dream, he is still full of it and attentive to his cue; he goes out of his way home to learn whether the play has been placed on the list. To save delay he suppresses his longing to 'discourse wonders' to the others; he hurries them off with a flood of instructions and last-minute ideas. On the stage he turns to the audience in his anxiety to put them right, and supply a hint as to what is coming; and even when supposedly prostrate in death his ears are open for further comments to correct.

In common with Dogberry (*Much Ado About Nothing*) and Launcelot Gobbo (*The Merchant of Venice*), Nick Bottom sprinkles his talk with amusing malapropisms and contradictory expressions. In fact, one suspects that he who could 'aggravate' a lion's voice as gently as any 'sucking dove' and mix up the senses as he does at the end of IV, 1 must have had a hand in composing the dialogue of *Pyramus and Thisbe* when it refers to the moon's 'sunny beams' and contains such lines as

I see a voice: now will I to the chink,
To spy and I can hear my Thisbe's face. (V, 1, 190–1)

Guild-plays were often the work of such men as Bottom the weaver. On the other hand, it is possible that he has not had the time to make himself word-perfect, and that these are slips as comically his as 'odious savours sweet'. He has a weakness for alliteration, whether of the ranting kind – 'The raging rocks' (I, 2) – or in such adaptations as 'Mounsieur Mustard-seed' and 'Cavalery Cobweb', and 'peck of provender'. Above all, he is a great talker; lest his garrulousness give them away, Titania bids her fairies, 'Tie up my love's tongue, bring him silently'.

Theseus

Out of this silence yet I pick'd a welcome.

In this 'renowned duke' can be seen a first sketch by Shakespeare of the warrior-king he was later to portray in *Henry V*. There are the same qualities, more faintly yet quite clearly outlined: prowess in battle, winning him a bride; a strict sense of justice, applied to high and low, now overruling the old courtier Egeus for the sake of his daughter's happiness, now giving place of honour to the wretched interlude of ignorant artisans because he sees in it a more genuine expression of loyalty than the more academic themes competing with it for performance; piety in the dutiful observance of religious ceremonies; a personal popularity which inspires the humblest of his subjects to strive to entertain him, and draws to his wedding the fairy rulers from their distant realm; a practical outlook, rather blind on the imaginative side, with a similar dislike to Henry's of 'these fellows of infinite tongue, that can rhyme themselves into ladies' favours' (*Henry V*, V, 2, 159–62).

Apart from giving Hermia time to reconsider her decision, he has nothing to do with the action of the play, for the plot has been resolved before Act IV, and in Act V he reappears to preside over what is almost an extended epilogue, bringing the different groups together for a final ensemble – the happily married couples 'full of joy and mirth', the actors excelling themselves in unconscious burlesque, and the fairies bestowing their blessings in song and dance.

To Theseus the action of the play is an episode in his wedding preparations, a mere lovers' dispute settled for him by a change of affection, not by the working of some magic power. The solution accords with his own sympathies, clearly shown by his tactfully leaving the lovers together at the outset, and in the end, when Demetrius returns to his first love, by his deliberately setting the law on one side.

Unlike the youthful Lysander and Demetrius, Theseus loves with the moderation of one to whom love takes its place among a number of other interests. He speaks of 'my Hippolyta' and not of 'goddess, nymph, perfect, divine'. He entertains his bride 'with pomp, with triumph, and with revelling' and magnanimously admits the two couples to an equal share in the ceremony.

His active life now belongs to the past; in his Greek incarnation he is himself an 'antique fable', having almost as many feats to his credit as his kinsman Hercules. The age of Pericles in Athens is remote enough, but Theseus belongs to a millennium earlier. He was the legendary founder of the city, his monument the Theseum being the most complete Greek temple in existence. A great warrior and administrator, he also had a bad reputation as a lover. He even deserted Ariadne, who saved him from the Minotaur by giving him the famous sword and ball of thread. His 'issue' was a son, Hippolytus, whose death he deliberately brought about out of jealousy; he died a tyrant's death. In Chaucer he is a 'duke' addicted to hunting who chances upon the two rivals with swords drawn.

Shakespeare has made of him a cultured 16th-century English nobleman, whose honours sit light upon him, and who is wise in the ways of the world; a benevolent autocrat who expects and receives implicit obedience, delights in stage shows and the pleasures of the chase and has a firm regard for those who serve him in the humblest capacity; a man of action who frets at delays, is intolerant of dreamers and regards drama as an empty pageant serving only to pass the time away. For him true satisfaction lies in the substance of this world, not in its shadows, the 'airy nothings' of the poet's imagination and the 'faint hymns' of barren renunciation in a cloister. He has no use for 'saucy and audacious eloquence'; he finds what he wants in 'tongue-tied simplicity'.

Hippolyta

'Tis strange, my Theseus, that these lovers speak of.

For one who must have been a ruthless female warrior, Theseus's bride is sensitive to the sufferings of others. Her expression, without her saying a word, indicates how sad she is over Hermia's predicament. She is ready to believe the lovers' story of their crossed loves; she is reluctant to watch the mechanicals making fools of themselves (it is to her 'the silliest stuff' and she quickly tires of the 'moon'); Pyramus's passion arouses what she calls 'pity' and she hopes Thisbe will not take so long over it. Hers is the passive part of a spectator; the only hint of her athletic background is her delight in the distant baying of a pack of hounds.

It is unlikely that the *Amazons* ever existed as such, but their fierce fight with the Greeks in the centre of Athens is part of the city's legendary history. Early historians were reluctant to let such a fascinating tribe disappear from their records; long years afterwards the sight of some long-haired Indians in South America, who had been taken for female warriors by some short-sighted Spaniards, gave the longest river in the world its name!

Oberon

What night-rule now about this haunted grove?

In contrast to the ruler of men, who judges calmly by the light of 'cool reason', is the 'King of Shadows', whose actions are inspired by passing whims. To get his own way, he plays a practical joke on his own royal partner; when he sees the result, however, he is full of pity for her. A kindly impulse leads him to send Puck to use the herb upon a mortal lover, and when his messenger mistakes one Athenian for another, he scolds him for his 'knaveries' and despatches the unrepentant mocker to spread a fog and separate the rivals.

His rule ends with cock-crow, though, unlike the ghosts of the unburied dead, he can disport himself in the early morning sunlight. Therefore he is anxious that, before he and his train 'trip after the night's shade', there shall be a general reconciliation and 'all things shall be peace'. He has watched Cupid in action, listened to the songs of mermaids and hunted with the shepherd love of Aurora.

Some of the finest lines in the play are Oberon's. His speeches, like those of Titania, are alive with poetic fantasy.

The fairies

Following darkness like a dream.

Shakespeare's creation of a fairy realm was something new on the English stage. As so often in his plays, he has succeeded in blending diverse elements into a living, satisfying whole. From medieval literature he has taken the 'fays' of human stature, able to cast spells and travel with the speed of thought, and made them sovereigns over a race of diminutive elves belonging to popular folklore.

Oberon and Titania converse with the dignity and eloquence of human kings and queens. Puck, on a lower plane, unable to see what Oberon can see, is yet a degree above the familiar hobgoblin, for he has the arrow-like swiftness necessary to an attendant upon Oberon. The fairies are associated in the audience's mind with a minuteness impossible to reproduce on the stage, even when their parts are taken by children. The fairy sovereigns are elemental by nature, their quarrels disturbing the seasons; their tiny followers hide in acorn-cups, wear coats of bats' wings, make fans of butterflies' wings, hang dew-drops in cowslip bells and make war on insects, newts and worms.

'Fairy time' is from midnight to cock-crow; its divisions are proportionately minute – Titania sends her retinue on a hunting expedition 'for the third part of a minute'. The fairies hold their revels by moonlight, now dancing in circles upon the well-known 'fairy rings', now sporting on distant shores. Their master and mistress, normally invisible to human eyes (it was considered fatal to catch sight of fairies, cf. *The Merry Wives of Windsor*, V, 5), are able to assume human form and be in love with mortals, as Titania formerly was with Theseus, and Oberon with Hippolyta.

Puck

I am that merry wanderer of the night.

Whereas his master is a handsome immortal spirit from the

distant Orient, Puck has just come from a nearby English village. His pranks are given in boastful detail by himself and admiringly by the fairy in Act II, Scene 1, perhaps as a preparation for the supreme prank played, deliberately but for no special reason, on Bottom. It is quite by accident that he complicates the lovers' relationships but he gets as much fun from their 'fond pageant' as if he had contrived it himself.

His two special gifts are (1) the power to assume any shape and imitate any sound, all familiar to a superstitious audience, and (2) the speed of Ariel, his more ethereal counterpart in *The Tempest*. The latter facility would explain his presence in Greece. For some obscure reason he was unable to see what Oberon saw (the arrow and the flower), but later was taken to see the wild pansy ('love-in-idleness') and remembered it when sent to fetch it. Also not clear is Shakespeare's purpose in putting into Puck's mouth words incompatible with his characteristic merry mischief. His role in Act III Scene 2 is varied: first he delivers an almost epic description of his mistress in love with a monster; one minute he utters a philosophic couplet about Fate and the next he announces Helena's arrival in his usual tripping lines. When swift action is needed to separate the lovers, first Oberon – and then, as if in emulation, Puck – employ poetic terms; he greets the approach of dawn with flesh-creeping lines that add an eerie touch to the audience's expectations of an imminent fight to the death. Thereafter all is swift action as he lures first one then the other on wearying goose-chases until they drop exhausted within yards of each other. Lastly he applies the remedy to Lysander and crows his way off stage with the proverbial cry, 'Jack shall have Jill'. It is the same English Puck who, when the airy sprites have executed their elaborate dance, makes his irresistible appeal to an English audience.

The lovers

The course of true love never did run smooth.

The characters of the lovers are only lightly sketched. This is necessary since their actions are in part determined by fairy means. *Demetrius* may be distinguished from *Lysander* by a more surly demeanour; in Act V he is more forward than his late rival in remarks upon the 'interlude', perpetrating puns and bandying 'conceits' with Theseus. *Helena* is tall, fair and gentle ('a dove'), *Hermia* short, dark and vixenish ('a raven'). Both the women are constant in their love; it is the men who change. In Shakespeare's plays woman's love is unaffected by reason and caprice alike. These two, however, differ from the heroines of later comedies in an absence of intellectual wit. Neither Beatrice nor Rosalind would have suffered the men to do all the talking in Act V.

The term 'characterless', as used by some critics, is unfair. They are four likeable young people caught in a love tangle. A close-knit schoolgirl friendship is shattered by a sudden confrontation, the women's passionate verbal duel being the climax of the play, while the men's fogbound armed search for each other ends in an anti-climax. Their conversation is not devoid of interest: perhaps in the modern view they lack depth because they are not self-centred or over-sexed, aggressive or malicious, fanatically or criminally inclined, in fact offering no kind of psychological problem for extended discussion.

The mechanicals

Hard-handed men that work in Athens here.

Classical stories were frequently presented in Elizabethan masques and pageants, and among the audiences would be little knots of guildsmen or villagers who would be seized with a desire to reproduce for themselves what they had seen and heard. The script and stage-effects would be their own work, and the performance would be thoroughly enjoyed by all the actors.

The resourcefulness of Quince's little band of aspirants to theatrical fame is shown by (1) their attempts at stage realism, which contrast so crudely with the dramatist's own appeal to the imagination of his audience through the medium of poetic suggestion and (2) their ability to write up a completely new text in a few hours! The proper explanation of this last point is, of course, that it is only one more of those discrepancies to be found in almost all of Shakespeare's plays, for he was supremely indifferent to minor inaccuracies that had no dramatic significance.

Bottom so dominates the scene that little individuality is left for the others, nor is it needed. *Quince*, the nominal producer, is probably older than the rest, rather querulous and given to correcting his juniors – though he himself is put right in IV, 2 by the very man he criticized in III, 1. Quince is more knowledgeable than they are, and presumably wrote the script, possibly with some dictation from Bottom! He gives in to Bottom on all points, except to insist that he must content himself with the lover's part.

The famous first part of the prologue, which Quince mispunctuates, is really a misplaced epilogue, probably inserted by Shakespeare as a humorous extra, to start the ball of witty comment rolling. *Flute*, in his own person as well as that of Thisbe, is an admirer of Bottom; he is told to conceal his stubbly chin behind a mask and speak as well as he can in a woman's voice – a typical thrust by the dramatist at one of the limitations of the stage of his day. *Snug* is 'slow of study', and, instead of giving his part 'extempore' with a single roar, has to master a speech explaining the obvious, namely that far from being a real lion, he is only a man in a lion's skin. That other 'noble beast', *Starveling*, burdened with lantern, thorn-bush and dog, is kept standing so long by the interruptions of the spectators that he flings the gist of his lines at them in the bluntest English. *Snout*, who is chiefly anxious that the audience should not be frightened by sword-play or a lion, is himself frightened in the wood by what he sees on Bottom's shoulders. For a detailed list of parts and actors, see note on Act V.

Style

Vocabulary

Shakespeare's vocabulary has been calculated to exceed fifteen thousand words, well ahead of his nearest competitor Milton, with eight thousand. Many of his words, once in everyday Elizabethan use, are now obsolete, e.g. 'coil' (trouble); the meanings of others have changed, e.g. 'amazed' (puzzled); some were even then archaic, but useful in poetry, e.g. 'eyne' (eyes). Shakespeare must have been an omnivorous reader with a comprehensive memory. Such a well-stocked mind, combined with great imaginative powers, enabled him not only to compose the dialogue of lifelike characters but also to create an impression of the setting and atmosphere in which they moved; whole passages have the substance of short poems, studded with literary allusions and topical references.

Description

His earlier manner was often daringly experimental as he tried out far-fetched analogies and intricate figures of speech. His 'middle period', as it has been called, struck an even balance between idea and expression; in his great tragedies powerful emotions and a wealth of imagery break the restraints of precise grammar, plain logic and metrical regularity to reach an eloquence beyond what had gone before and rarely equalled since.

In *A Midsummer Night's Dream*, one of the 'earlier' comedies at the beginning of this middle period, his style is some way from maturity but has the freshness that belongs to the open air, suffused with the witchcraft that haunts the woodland when the moon is up. It is concerned in the main with the jealousies, the misunderstandings and the strange infatuations of youthful love. There are arguments and accusations, pleas for pity, scornful rejoinders, threats of personal violence. The language is descriptive and suited to the moment rather than figurative, simple and natural when expressing the genuine emotions of love and hatred, artificial and extravagant when spoken under the spell of herbally induced devotion.

Dialogue

The dialogue is well adapted to the characters: the aristocratic tone of the Duke, the querulousness of old Egeus, the fussy stage-managerisms of Quince, the earthy humour of Puck and the inexhaustible self-sufficiency of Bottom, equal to all emergencies.

Influences

Assiduous researchers into Shakespeare's alleged sources will continue to find similarities of idea and phrasing, and often identical words in particular contexts. Kenneth Muir has found numerous parallels in a poem *Of the Silkworms, and their Flies*, by Thomas Mouffet, which Shakespeare may have seen in manuscript (See *Further reading*). Whether unconscious 'echoes' or what we would call downright plagiarism today, this was common practice in Shakespeare's time and whatever he took he made peculiarly his own. In one earlier version of *Pyramus and Thisbe*, a stage direction makes Bottom, at the point of expiry, open and shut his eyes: did this prompt his spontaneous resurrection in the *Dream*?

Shakespeare owed something to Marlowe's 'mighty line' (blank verse), and parallels have been detected between his style and that of this friend and almost exact contemporary (1564–93). The titles of two of Marlowe's plays and of a poem are echoed in our play: *Dido, Queen of Carthage* (I, 1, 173), *The Jew of Malta* (III, 1, 90) and *Hero and Leander*, translated by Bottom as 'Helen and Limander' (V, 1, 194). In the poem, begun by Marlowe and finished by Chapman, we find:

Love's arrows with the golden head (cf. I, 1, 170)
crown'd with odorous roses, white as snow (cf. III, 1, 78)
Night, deep-drench'd in misty Acheron (cf. III, 2, 357)
Abandon fruitless virginity . . .
Then shall you most resemble Venus' nun (cf. I, 1, 73)
Who taught thee rhetoric to deceive a maid? (cf. II, 2, 52)

Further tempting examples may be found in the works of John

Lyly and others of the group of 'University Wits'; a large number of contemporary plays perished unrecorded, possible sources for suitable words or original ideas. In the decade before *A Midsummer Night's Dream* romantic love was a universal topic and much of the language was common property.

If Shakespeare's actor friends had not taken the trouble to produce the first Folio of his plays, how much poorer would our dictionaries of quotations be today! One reason, perhaps, why we admire the aptness and especially the naturalness of his diction is that generations of familiarity with the texts of his plays, as declaimed from the stage or perused in the study, have had a lasting influence on our language.

General questions plus questions on related topics for coursework/examinations on other books you may be studying

1 Discuss Shakespeare's use of the supernatural in *A Midsummer Night's Dream*.
Suggested notes for essay answer:

Fairy world a novel and successful experiment – atmosphere of romantic East made credible by co-existence with and contrast with everyday workmen – fairies dance and sing, Athenians struggle with play production;

Problem of size – human dimensions and diminutive reconciled by Shakespeare's poetic imagination – parallel between lovers' quarrels and that of the fairy sovereigns;

Fairies invisible to all but Bottom, who takes on his new, not self-imposed role with characteristic confidence – his holding court in a supernatural setting the high point of the comedy;

Puck, embodying contemporary superstition and shown in his natural woodland setting associated with Greek myth – untrue to character, is given the speed of Ariel;

Limited use of supernatural in Shakespeare – Ghost in *Hamlet* and Weird Sisters in *Macbeth* concerned with motives of main characters – Puck and Ariel (*Tempest*) serve masters with supernatural powers – their orders shape events on the stage;

The magic flower and its antidote are representative of a body of herbal lore, some secret and mischievous – given appearance of magic power by being fetched from a great distance – lovers try to explain what has happened;

Theseus's matter-of-fact attitude to things that may take place in the dark is framework to Shakespeare's fairy world, the 'truth' of which is assessed by the reaction of the human audience.

2 How great is Shakespeare's success in blending three plots into one comedy?

3 Account for Puck's mistakes and show how he made up for them.

4 How many chance encounters can you mention? Give a short account of each.

5 In how many different parts of the wood does the action take place? Say briefly what happened at each place.

6 Put yourself in the place of one of the lovers and tell the story of his or her bewilderment as it might be recounted to Theseus.

7 Write a description of the Fairies and show how Puck differs from the rest.

8 How do you think the characters should be grouped on the stage at the entrance of Puck in IV, 1?

9 Which character derives most entertainment from the behaviour of others? Justify your choice.

10 Make Bottom relate his dream to his companions (with touches of his characteristic style, if you can).

11 If you had been in Quince's place, how would you have improved the performance of the play, allowing for the conditions of the time?

12 Compare and contrast Hermia and Helena in appearance and in character.

13 How far can you distinguish between Lysander and Demetrius?

14 Which scene do you think provides the best comedy? Give your reasons.

15 Sketch the character of Egeus and explain his absence from the wedding.

16 Make a comparison of the functions of Theseus and Oberon.

17 Write about any book you have read recently which has a rural or country setting and say what it contributed to your appreciation of the story.

18 Write an appreciation of a grotesque or ridiculous scene in your chosen book.

19 How important is the theme of deception in any book you are studying? Show what part it has in the plot of the story.

20 Give an account of any supernatural elements in a book you know well.

21 Write about the treatment of love and romance in a book you are studying.

22 Examine the presentation of fantasy and its effects in terms of plot or character in one of your books.

23 Indicate the various types of humour in a play, novel or story you know well.

24 Bring out the various aspects of an author's style in any one of his/her books.

25 Compare and contrast any character in *A Midsummer Night's Dream* with any character in one of your chosen books.

Further reading

The Arden Shakespeare: A Midsummer Night's Dream, edited by Harold F. Brooks (Methuen 1979)

Critics on Shakespeare, W. T. Andrews (ed.), (Allen & Unwin 1952).

Narrative and Dramatic Sources of Shakespeare, Geoffrey Bullough (Vol. I, Routledge 1957).

William Shakespeare, E. K. Chambers (Clarendon Press 1930).

The Sources of Shakespeare's Plays, Kenneth Muir (Methuen 1977).

Shakespeare, Allardyce Nicoll (Methuen 1952).

Shakespeare, Walter Raleigh (Macmillan 1907).

Shakespeare's Imagery, Caroline Spurgeon (CUP 1953).

Life in Shakespeare's England, J. D. Wilson (Macmillan 1913).

Brodie's Notes

TITLES IN THE SERIES

D. H. Lawrence	**The Rainbow**
D. H. Lawrence	**Sons and Lovers**
D. H. Lawrence	**Women in Love**
Harper Lee	**To Kill a Mockingbird**
Laurie Lee	**Cider with Rosie**
Christopher Marlowe	**Dr Faustus**
Arthur Miller	**The Crucible**
Arthur Miller	**Death of a Salesman**
John Milton	**Paradise Lost**
Robert C. O'Brien	**Z for Zachariah**
Sean O'Casey	**Juno and the Paycock**
George Orwell	**Animal Farm**
George Orwell	**1984**
J. B. Priestley	**An Inspector Calls**
J. D. Salinger	**The Catcher in the Rye**
William Shakespeare	**Antony and Cleopatra**
William Shakespeare	**As You Like It**
William Shakespeare	**Hamlet**
William Shakespeare	**Henry IV Part I**
William Shakespeare	**Julius Caesar**
William Shakespeare	**King Lear**
William Shakespeare	**Macbeth**
William Shakespeare	**Measure for Measure**
William Shakespeare	**The Merchant of Venice**
William Shakespeare	**A Midsummer Night's Dream**
William Shakespeare	**Much Ado about Nothing**
William Shakespeare	**Othello**
William Shakespeare	**Richard II**
William Shakespeare	**Romeo and Juliet**
William Shakespeare	**The Tempest**
William Shakespeare	**Twelfth Night**
George Bernard Shaw	**Pygmalion**
Alan Sillitoe	**Selected Fiction**
John Steinbeck	**Of Mice and Men and The Pearl**
Jonathan Swift	**Gulliver's Travels**
Dylan Thomas	**Under Milk Wood**
Alice Walker	**The Color Purple**
W. B. Yeats	**Selected Poetry**

ENGLISH COURSEWORK BOOKS

Terri Apter	**Women and Society**
Kevin Dowling	**Drama and Poetry**
Philip Gooden	**Conflict**
Philip Gooden	**Science Fiction**
Margaret K. Gray	**Modern Drama**
Graham Handley	**Modern Poetry**
Graham Handley	**Prose**
Graham Handley	**Childhood and Adolescence**
R. J. Sims	**The Short Story**